Other bo

How to St

How to Be a Good Atheist

NICK HARDING

OLDCASTLE BOOKS

This edition published in 2007 by Oldcastle Books Ltd,
P.O. Box 394, Harpenden, Herts, AL5 1XJ
www.oldcastlebooks.com

Series Editor Nick Rennison
Proofs & Index Rickard Howard

A CIP catalogue record for this book is available from the British Library.

ISBN 10: 1–84243–237–0
ISBN 13: 978–1–84243–237–2

2 4 6 8 10 9 7 5 3 1

Typeset by Avocet Typeset, Chilton, Aylesbury, Bucks
Printed and bound in Great Britain by J.H. Haynes & Co Ltd, Sparkford, Somerset

Acknowledgements

For font dodgers everywhere – there are more of us than we think.

For her compassion and love, Andrea Bertorelli who patiently listens to my settee-based lectures on the subject. Dr. Jerry 'Stubby' Kaye, Nick Richards and Tim Calvert, fellow non-believers. Sean Martin who puts the boot in from the other direction. Ion Mills for the first rungs up the long ladder, the creators of *Family Guy*, The Pythons and XTC, who were Jumping in Gomorrah and religion free.

For their continuing inspiration: Richard Dawkins, Charles Darwin, Carl Sagan, Michael Shermer, James Randi, Thomas Paine, AC Grayling, Christopher Hitchens, Sam Harris, Derren Brown, Daniel Dennett, Douglas E. Krueger, George H. Smith and to the freethinkers of the Enlightenment – voices of reason all.

Special thanks to Richard Dawkins for his generosity.

Libertas per scientiam naturae rerum.

Tantum religio potuit suadere malorum...
(Such are the heights of wickedness to which
men are driven by religion...)
Lucretius, *De Rerum Natura*

*Wandering in a vast forest at night, I have only
a faint light to guide me. A stranger appears and
says to me: 'My friend, you should blow out your
candle in order to find your way more clearly.'
This stranger was a theologian.*
Diderot, *Addition aux pensées philosophiques*

God is my favourite fictional character
Homer Simpson

*'What about us atheists? Why should we have to listen
to that sectarian turmoil?'*
Monty Python, *Bells, Contractual Obligation Album.*

Contents

Introduction

How to be an atheist? Well, for a start, the answer is rather easy. Stop believing in any nonsense that has not one scrap of evidence to back it up. Like a deity. Religion is an obstruction to clear thinking, the destruction of rationality. So, in order to think straight, give up any idea of the big ghost. Rationality is far preferable to irrationality. How could it not be? The whole religious enterprise is somewhat silly and it's the insanity of religion that irritates atheists… we are worth more than that, so…

Be a non-believer.

Atheism – Greek *a*, without, *theos*, god = godless

Throughout the long and troubled history of religion, that buzzing wasp's nest of baseless vitriol, the one constant crown of thorns in its ecumenical backside has been non-belief, i.e. atheism. Nothing else summons up so much fire and brimstone from the depths of ignorance than that one seven-letter word. The individual who has chosen to ignore the absurdities and innate contradictions of theological teachings by exercising free thought has been criticised, ostracised and even burnt at the stake for knowing that religious faith is a non-starter. That same individual who has chosen a life free of theistic tyranny has also had to face some pretty daft and lame accusations directed at him by the faithful, from cavorting with Old Nick to absence of morals, from encouraging nudity through to mental illness, political subversion and revolution. 'What have atheists not done to humanity?', comes the cry from frenetic bigots. People are swift to denounce atheism for what it isn't rather than what it is – they simply don't know what disbelief entails. But their religion, (from the Latin word *religare*, meaning 'to bind', a definition which sums things up rather nicely) has itself a lot to defend – a lot of contradictory, nasty, bloodthirsty and very silly things as it happens. Their last redoubt is 'faith', the idealistic notion that insubstantial hope and wishful thinking (which is all religion comes down to anyway) will see a believer through.

God is nothing more than nature viewed in anthropomorphic terms. God is nature in man's image. Children ascribe emotions to inanimate objects and, in many individuals; this practice stays with them into adulthood, when it is called religion. Also the notion that we call a god, 'father', or a goddess, 'mother' is more revealing than perhaps first appears, especially in Freudian terms. Religion treats people like children and tends to encourage the mind to stay in an infantile state. Atheism is the mind 'growing up'.

Religion is like that old joke, which has numerous variations:

> *'By wearing this bright hat, I keep lions away.'*
> *'But there aren't any lions in Romford.'*
> *'There you go, it works...'*

Recently theistic apologists like Alister McGrath have attempted to beat us limply over our collective heads with the wet sock of falsehood, claiming that Richard Dawkins and other atheists are horribly wrong. Hence the title of McGrath's peculiar and (thankfully) slim book *The Dawkins Delusion*. Dawkins is not wrong nor is he shallow, as writer and columnist AN Wilson once described him in a juvenile Daily Mail article. If anything theists are shallow, preferring the perfunctory and trivial world of silly rituals, insubstantial doctrines and fantasy realms that are so flimsy they can be swept away by papal whim. McGrath, a one-time atheist who gave up thinking to turn to faith, has convinced himself that atheism is on the decline. (It isn't.) By doing this he reveals that he prefers a world of theistic despotism and repression to free thought and reason. He thinks we should all bow before the supernatural as slaves to ghosts. All he has done is sell himself to the devil of religious defeatism.

Literary critics who use a*d hominem* attacks when launching feeble broadsides at the likes of Dawkins or atheists in general reveal the fact that they are both anti-reason and anti-rationality. All critics of atheism are swift to lumber it with the epithet 'bombastic' as well as blaming it for all the horrors of the twentieth century. This is just nonsense. The great conflicts of the twentieth century were not down to atheism – if anything they were the result of the 'army states', a creation of nineteenth century European imperialism and of course the bellicose tendencies of religion.

What is it about atheism that sparks so much antagonism? It is, after all, only the refusal to accept silly beliefs about the non-existent. It should be, by all rights, regarded as what it is, the highest form of rationality and reason to which humanity can aspire. Instead, it suffers at the wringing hands and frothing mouths of hypocritical priests, journalists, politicians and film-makers who make ridiculous claims that atheism is responsible for the perceived moral decline and social destruction of our world. The fact is that we have had religion, in all its forms, for millennia and it has proved useless in steering morality but religious apologists are selectively blind to this.

When the Archbishop of York, John Sentamu, a man who makes a protest about an illegal war by sleeping in a tent in front of his altar, utters his vapid and tiresome claims that society is falling apart because of atheists and (horror of horrors!) liberals, his personal scapegoats, he should not be allowed to get away with it. Sentamu and others should use their dictionaries to look up the meaning of liberal, i.e. open minded, generous, abundant, unprejudiced, progressive, favouring individual liberty, demo-cratic and so on. (He may, of course, be criticising Liberals with a capital L who, as Sam Harris shows in his book *The End of Faith*, have been guilty of tolerating the excesses of religion.) Sentamu seems to forget that we have had around 1,200 years, since at least the time of Alfred the Great, in which Christianity has been the national religion. When exactly, during this period, was there a golden age when Britain shone like a beacon as a glorious example of an upright, moral, crime-free society? In fact, when has any country that claims religion to be its focus? The answer is, of course, never. As if to contradict himself, the Archbishop of York has made claims, more recently, that we are heading towards 'illiberal secularism', whatever that may be. If we are this is due;

in part to the bigoted views his fellow theists have about homo-sexuals and women priests – prehistoric ideas and baseless taboos that are starting to tear the Anglican Church apart. And, when this happens, we're all going to hell! This is medieval and archaic thinking writ large. Of course, the Bishop and his chums could make the vacuous statement that, without Christianity, the world might have been a much worse place but the truth is that theism, in all its forms, has been responsible for endless bloodshed throughout history. It's rather difficult to mount a defence of faith as a redoubt of decency. We are better off without religion.

Theists are very good at pointing their holier-than-thou fingers at the rest of us and are quick to blame everyone but themselves for the way of the world. (The term 'theist' will be used throughout this book to mean anyone who believes in a deity or who adheres to a religion whatever form that takes.) All they see is mortal corruption and godless immorality. How negative. How dull and, more importantly, how narrow-minded. Certainly, the human world is not perfect but, god or no god, it never has been. Theists tell us that the bible, or some other so-called holy book, is the only source of moral teaching but then they busily pick and choose which bits to accept and which bits to reject as just metaphor. If they can do this so easily, does this not suggest that people already have an inbuilt moral code and that they don't need a religious screed to teach them what's right and wrong? Surely, they must have if, working counter to the wishes of their capricious deity, they can decide which bits of biblical morality can be used and which can't. Or is this some form of rebellion?

What prompts theists to believe, if they survive a plane crash in which a hundred or more fellow passengers have perished, that they have been singled out for divine protection? Why didn't their god help everyone else to survive? Why did he allow the plane to crash? Why did he allow other theists on the plane to die? Come to think of it, where is this all-powerful being during innumerable other disasters that war, earthquake and tsunami create annually around the globe, disasters in which the lives of countless innocent people are lost? Most of them believers in a god...

Why go on trips to Lourdes to seek a cure for some ailment? Shouldn't a benevolent all-seeing deity be able to cure the afflicted without an uncomfortable coach trip to France? Why did god allow a person to be struck with some medical condition in the first place? More importantly, shouldn't all the faithful be cured of their particular condition? Shouldn't there be a long line of joyous people casting away their walking sticks, zimmer frames and wheelchairs in the carparks? Why do people from all round the world travel to this place and come away disappointed yet still don't seem to be that bothered? They simply continue to believe that the place has curative properties and that it works 'miracles' (nothing more than misinterpretations of natural phenomena or outright lies and fantasy), despite all the evidence to the contrary.

While the white man was running riot across the New World, a Navajo chieftain had a vision from his god who told him to gather the tribes and have a dance to see off the invader. The Navajo did so. The palefaces kept on coming. Despite the failure of his god's plan, that Navajo went right on believing in his sky spirit. Reality cannot change a theist's mind whatever his particular belief system.

In the face of constant disappointment and a blinkered view of reality, theists just continue to believe in the preposterous idea of a deity. The ghastly misanthropic millenarians and their ilk are the ones guiltiest of harbouring such wide-eyed optimism – if it can be called such – in their desire for elitist 'rapture'. As Robert Ehrlich wrote in an edition of eSkeptic, Wednesday, 2 May 2007:

> On occasion religious figures also make predictions, most notably about the end of the world, but I am unfamiliar with any example where the failure of the world to end on schedule caused a reassessment of the religious leaders in their fundamental beliefs. Instead, the holy man and the faithful sometimes make some recalculations, and come up with a new date for the end of the world, or else give up trying with their faith unshaken – for that is the nature of faith which requires no evidence to justify it, yet somehow paradoxically it craves confirming evidence when it can get it. Hence today it is a matter of legitimate concern that with biblical fundamentalists in control of nuclear arsenals an acceptance of biblical prophecy concerning Armageddon and certain events in the Middle East might well lead to self-fulfilling prophecies.

And people have the cheek to moan about atheists? That last sentence should fill any right-thinking individual with a genuine sense of dread. There are theists who desperately want this to happen and are happy to support and indeed encourage war in the Middle East to bring about the second coming. It beggars belief that thousands might have to die to support a myth.

If god is omnipotent and omniscient, why is there so much corruption and indeed *evil* in the world? Evil, it should be said, that is often perpetrated by those who claim to serve their god. Just where is god in all this? Why the silence? Why has he allowed millions to die in his name? Why, if he created all of us out of love, is he so enraged by same-sex marriages and women priests? Shouldn't he take some responsibility for all this wanton destruction and hatred? Where exactly is god? Has he given up on us? Where is the sense in believing in a deity who claims to be all-loving and benevolent but who has created a hell into which he'll cast you if you are a non-believer? Why did he create us so that we could worship him? Isn't that a dictatorship, a kind of enslavement? Surely, at the very least, a bad case of narcissism? Why, when devout theists, people who actually believe he's there, pray, do they receive nothing in return for their efforts? Why do their heartfelt requests go unheard? Does he care?

Or is it, as is undoubtedly the case, that he simply doesn't exist?

Has religion sold us a big fat shiny celestial lemon? And are some people sucking too hard on it, hence their sour and miserable expressions? Well, atheists think so. Actually, they don't think so. They know so. The popularity of books like Richard Dawkins' *The God Delusion,* Sam Harris' *The End of Faith*, the recently published *God: The Failed Hypothesis* by physicist Victor Stenger and Christopher Hitchens' *God Is Not Great: How Religion Poisons Everything* supports the welcome notion that more and more people think so too. These writers, prominent among a growing number of anti-theist authors, continue to push the debate to the fore, much to the alarm of apoplectic and vitriolic clergymen up and down the land. The paranoid Archbishop of Canterbury is even convinced that there's an atheist conspiracy in which the publishing world is a player! Books like these – and there are more each year – increase the pressure on theists, forcing them to respond with ever-more bitter and empty attacks on atheism. Usually, these take the form of scare tactics – appeals to people's fear of so-called moral decline. (In fact, if you compare the present to the past, you'll see that things are better now than they have ever been. At least we no longer hang people or burn them at the stake.) Theists also make great play with the supposedly negative politics of their opponents and utter ridiculous and clumsy statements that atheists are Nazis. Sometimes they allege simultaneously that they are the polar opposite – communists. Like politicians, theists claim, you're safer with us. But it's a lie.

We're worse off with religion. As AC Grayling writes in *What Is Good?*:

> *Most human progress has occurred in the face*
> *of religious reaction, and most human suffering*
> *other than that caused by disease or other natural*
> *evils has been the result of religion-inspired conflict*
> *and religion-based oppression.*

Atheism has come a long way in terms of acceptance in society, although many still despise it, thereby revealing only their deep ignorance of what it actually is. Pierre Bayle, French philosopher, critic and Cartesian fideistic sceptic, argued as long ago as 1681 that atheists could quite easily form a decent society. He also said that, despite its claims to the contrary, religion was next to useless as a moral control. The first openly atheistic book was chemist Matthew Turner's *Answer to Dr Priestley's Letter to a Philosophical Unbeliever* from 1782. It was followed by Shelley's *The Necessity of Atheism* in 1811. Both works were roundly denounced. With a typical display of intolerance, theists saw to it that Shelley was swiftly booted out of Oxford for his non-belief.

Literature has less of an anti-atheist stance than was once the case – unless, of course, you look at those theist and creationist books which are full of meaningless, infantile twaddle – but it's been a long hard slog for atheism to reach the position it is now in. In the early part of the twentieth century, even standard reference books like the Harmsworth and Chambers Encyclopaedias were quite open in their dismissals of the subject. Today there is a broader acceptance. It is correct to say that now atheism has a genuine chance to express itself in the written word without fear of fiery retribution. None the less it still has a long way to go. Most libraries in this country have shelves heaving with theistic '*truths*' but readers are hard pushed to find a few books on disbelief. European society has softened to the idea of atheism but, in America, it's still a minority position under constant attack by bible-bashing bigots. As for atheism in the Middle East – rare, if non-existent!

As late as the early twentieth century atheists in America were not allowed to testify in court, which meant they were put at a severe legal disadvantage. The obtuse and facetious reasoning was that, because atheists do not believe in the reward of an afterlife, they could not be expected to tell the truth in court. In some parts of the United States they are still refused jobs, vilified, denounced and have to retreat into enclaves. There are also ongoing investigations into the abuse of atheists in the US military.

These attacks are, of course, nothing new and theists still use the same fruitless and redundant arguments they have employed for over a thousand years. The statement, for example, that atheism causes social collapse is outmoded, demeaning and wrong. There is no evidence to back it up but god-botherers still regurgitate it, usually in the pages of right-wing newspapers or church sermons, convinced they have trumped the atheists' aces. In all their arguments, the god-fearing have brought no new evidence to the table to support their claims and whenever rational arguments are laid before the feet of theists they resort to tired and meaningless rebuttals.

With atheism, it is often claimed, there is no morality. So atheism destroys morality, does it? Far from it. Religion puts morality in the realm of the supernatural. Atheism brings it back down to earth. To quote George H. Smith in *Atheism: The Case Against God*: 'Atheism, however, is not the destruction of morality; it is the destruction of supernatural morality. Likewise, atheism is not the destruction of happiness and love; it is the destruction of the idea that love and happiness can be achieved only in another world.' Men, of course, wrote the bible so there are bound to be some moral lessons in it but to claim all its morality comes from the sky is idiotic. Man created god and therefore man developed morality. It's that simple.

In its millions of years on the evolutionary trail, how did humanity survive in a world before Christianity, Buddhism, Judaism and Islam, all of which claim there is no morality but their own? Spectacularly well. So, doesn't that mean we can live quite happily without 'supernatural morality'? Without question. Doesn't that also mean that morality is inbuilt? Yes. If, before organised religions, we were only immoral savages, why didn't we wipe ourselves out? It's typical of theists and their racism that early articulate peoples were once perceived as immoral savages. This kind of thinking was later transported all over the British Empire and so-called 'Christian morality' was inflicted on indigenous populations who had been managing quite happily without it for thousands of years. The same is true today of elements of US foreign policy. Or think about the so-called morality of the Catholic Church that denies the use of condoms in the developing world that would help stop the spread of AIDS. Millions are doomed to suffer because of idiotic dogma.

Theism is not the source of morality, or indeed ethics, and, whatever theists say, atheism is steeped in morality…

Perhaps, atheism is nihilistic then?

It certainly is not. Atheism allows us to cast off any delusions we have about reality and our place in the universe. Atheists see things as they are. If the universe is amoral – and it is – then so be it. In contrast, ideas of original sin and predestination are nonsensical and the notion, common to most theists, that purpose in life means slavery to a supernatural dictator is idiotic. There is more nihilism in mental domination than in rational thought.

But what of the accusations that atheists can't lead meaningful lives? That happiness is denied them? That goodness can only be found by behaving like a fawning supplicant and kneeling at the feet of some slave-driving divine presence, benevolent only in his PR, who offers cheesy rewards if his bidding is done but eternal hell if it is not. That the Bible, Koran, or any religious book, is the only source of a moral code? How can we explain the Christian morality of President George Bush Jnr. and ex-Prime Minister Tony Blair who claim belief in the almighty but are seemingly unmoved by the half a million deaths that have occurred in the disastrous invasion of Iraq? How is that *Christian*? Or consider the piety of an Islamic suicide bomber. How can men and women blow themselves up in the name of their god and believe they are doing 'good work'? There are plenty of other clearly immoral theists, which means that religion cannot be the universal, ethical fix-all it claims to be. Shouldn't religion vaccinate people against wrongdoing? Surely theists in all their guises should be beyond reproach but they never are. Even the saintly Mother Teresa had a whole array of idiotic ideas (see Christopher Hitchens' *The Missionary Position: Mother Teresa in Theory and Practice*). If even the highly religious behave badly, then does that not mean that religion is pretty useless as a moral guide? It is nonsense to claim that belief in a god makes you automatically a better person. The opposite is often the case. Good and evil do not exist as defined artefacts of the material world. Good and evil do not operate like gravity or magnetism as identifiable forces in nature. Reality is amoral and it is we, both theists and atheists, who create morality.

In fact, atheists have a more rigorous moral system than the religious.

Why do some commentators (usually in the press) assume that those who believe in fairy tales are better than those who do not? Why are atheists seen as lacking and as lesser individuals? All they have done is rid themselves of belief in inane falsehoods. How is it theists think they're better than anyone else?

Why do atheists get such a bad press when it is men and women who believe in one god or another that wreak so much havoc around the world on a daily basis while continuing to decry non-believers as immoral? Why is their concept of atheism so skewed? But every denouncement of atheism is a hollow pursuit...

> *I can indeed hardly see how anyone ought to*
> *wish Christianity true; for if so the plain language*
> *of the text seems to show that the men who do not*
> *believe, and this would include my father, brother*
> *and almost all my best friends, will be everlastingly*
> *punished. And this is a damnable doctrine.*
>
> Charles Darwin, *Autobiography*

This book, because of limitations of space, is a brief introduction to the subject and should not be seen as an exhaustive guide. For further reading, see the Bibliography (Must-Have Books in an Atheist's Library) below. Other must-read books are mentioned in relation to a particular topic. Dates, to avoid confusion also use the standard BC and AD format.

What is Atheism?

Atheism is based upon a materialist philosophy, which holds that nothing exists but natural phenomena. There are no supernatural forces or entities, nor can there be any. Nature simply exists.

Madalyn Murray O'Hair, founder and president of American Atheists.

I believe in the religion of reason – the gospel of this world; in the development of the mind, in the accumulation of intellectual wealth, to the end that man may free himself from superstitious fear, to the end that he may take advantage of the forces of nature to feed and clothe the world.

Robert Ingersoll, Why I Am an Agnostic.

Despite efforts by theistic apologists to level the accusation that it is just another faith-based position, atheism, by its very nature, cannot be labelled a belief. To call atheism a *faith* is an oxymoronic statement. It is the absence of belief in deities or the childish idea that there are supernatural forces that control human existence. One cannot possess absence of faith or belief by having faith in atheism. Atheism can be seen as the opposite of theism but this is not always so. Some freethinkers do not like to be called atheists as, by definition, this means that there is theism and one must therefore accept the preposterous idea that there is a god (or gods) to deny. This is a perfectly understandable position to take. Contrary to what theologians claim, atheism is neither a cult nor a religion.

The basic argument is simple. Theists state categorically that a deity (or deities) exists; atheists say there is no such thing. Of course, it is for the theist to prove his or her position not the atheist. The atheist asks to be shown just one jot of evidence for the existence of god and has yet to see any. Without evidence of any kind it is impossible to make a judgement as to the veracity of theist claims. In fact, it is clear that the theist position is becoming more and more untenable as time passes. Atheism is the most logical stance to take. It provides a baseline of reason, the bedrock of thought. If we have preconceived ideas about a subject, in this case the existence of god, they will bias any investigation into it. Misconceptions of reality convince certain theists, the creationists, that the world really was formed in six days. They have gone to the subjects of earth history, geology and Darwinian evolution with their minds tainted and sullied by biblical myths that are read as fact. No matter what they see, theists will reject any empirical evidence that does not fit into their worldview. Evolution is wrong because it counters the biblical story of Adam and Eve. Geology is false because it proves the Earth is 4.6 billion years old and not 6,000 years – a figure originally reached in the seventeenth century by totting up all the bearded begetting that goes on in the bible.

In many respects becoming an atheist means adopting clarity of thought. For that reason, it must be seen as the highest aspiration of human consciousness. Atheism, by its very nature, represents mental freedom.

We despise dictators and tyrants yet we are asked by the godfearing to prostrate ourselves before a capricious despotic ghost and beg forgiveness. We are told that prayer works. How? Surely an omnipotent deity can see, know and sense all anyway. Why pray? We are taught the nonsense that we are all tainted by original sin and thus all of us are damned by the actions of a mythological character – the sins of non-existent ancestors are visited upon us. What have the theists ever done for us? They have led us down the biggest garden path in history. They have taken us down a cul-de-sac of thought and brought us to a complete and utter dead end in morality and ethics. We really have been sold a celestial lemon.

Atheism as a general belief can be broken down into a number of different positions. It can be divided into two basic standpoints. In the broad version of atheism, people simply do not accept the basic premise of theism; in the narrower and more determined position, they believe that the theistic position is not only misguided but actively wrong. Sometimes this is called 'fundamentalist atheism'. (The concepts of fundamentalism and atheism should not really be mixed but critics and theistic apologists like to label the extreme end of atheism as 'fundamental'. See *Defending Atheism* below.) These positions are also known as *implicit atheism* – the absence of theistic belief without a conscious rejection of it – and *explicit atheism* – the absence of theistic belief due to a conscious rejection of it.

Some prefer to break atheism down into five different subsets for a more specific analysis. A dogmatic atheist may be at odds with, say, a sceptical atheist but they are all part and parcel of the same thing.

The subsets are:

Dogmatic Atheism – No god. Critics call this a 'fundamentalist' position.

Sceptical Atheism – The mind is incapable of discovering if there is a god or not.

Critical Atheism – Evidence for theism is inadequate.

Philosophical Atheism – Failure to find any evidence for existence of god in the universe.

Speculative Atheism – Kant's position, wherein it is impossible to demonstrate existence of god.

With dogmatic atheism we see disbelief at its most hardcore. This is a perfectly understandable position to take. Freethinkers who take a long, hard look at the world around them realise that there can be no god. Where's the evidence? Why, after all this time, is there not one maker's name under a stone, a label that says © God, or even the slightest suggestion that this 'god malarkey', to quote writer and broadcaster Jonathan Meades, has any truth in it? As time passes and scientific understanding of the universe grows – often in the face of rabid anti-science, either from the left where some deny DNA and evolution because it suggests social Darwinism and eugenics or from the religious right who deny science because it treads on all their holier-than-thou toes and makes a mockery of the bogus twaddle that is creationism – it becomes more and more unlikely that there is a super-intelligent ghost running the show. Biologists like Richard Dawkins, known by some as 'Darwin's Rottweiler', can illustrate the natural world in biological terms without the need for the divine spark and physicists like Victor Stenger can show the same for the quantum universe. Both hold up a spotlight into the shadows and state with confidence, *well I can't see him...*

And they are far from alone.

Sceptical atheism may one day become redundant. In many respects, it already is. The advances in scientific discovery within the disciplines of neuroscience are making great strides in understanding the processes that operate within the 3lbs of grey matter called the brain. Susan Blackmore and others can now show that the personality within is nothing more than a fiction. There is no one inside looking out. There is no 'me', 'I' or 'you'. Consciousness is a by-product of the constant buzz of neuro-processing. If this is so, then faith is, at best, an ephemeral chemical spectre.

So, where is this god in whom the theists believe? Who is he?

> God was sitting on his ass in Nowhere, since at that time there was not even a universe, for hundreds of millions of years without an idea in his head, picking his nose and farting, when suddenly he became bored one moment in particular and said, in clear Hebrew, "From nothing I will create something," and he created the entire universe (whatever that may be) for the express purpose of creating you in his own image, complete down to the belly button.

Madalyn Murray O'Hair,
discourse entitled *Fundamentalist*

There's absolutely no evidence for a divine creator. When looking at how the natural world is constructed, critical atheists can see nothing that lends weight to the notion that it was all the work of some lonely creator. Nor can any other variety of atheist. There is an intellectual paucity to creationism or its latest reincarnation 'intelligent design' (often described as 'creationism in a cheap tuxedo' and about as intelligent as theism gets, which isn't very intelligent). Intelligent design is a conceptual dead end but it is often cited by hardcore theists as 'proof' as they make demands that politicians and educationalists submit to their propaganda. With nothing to back up their arguments, they resort to creating ghastly theme parks in which Stone Age children play with Tyrannosaurus Rex pets or reconstructing large-scale models of Noah's Ark complete with an animatronic Noah. Some woefully ridiculous illustrations of the Ark, such as that seen in the madhouse Institute of Creation Research Museum, now have dinosaurs in stalls surrounded by lions, lambs and amoeba.

To show the absurdity of trying to turn a myth into a science, one has only to consider the realities of fitting two each of millions of species, let alone their food, into a boat 450 by 75 by 45 feet. Consider the logistics of feeding and watering and cleaning up after all those animals.

Michael Shermer,
Why People Believe Weird Things.

Indeed. But creationists continue to promote this simplistic and infantile view that somehow all the animals of the world could be contained within a big boat. Not only that, they reinterpret certain facets of the myth in an attempt to make it workable. Not all animals went into the Ark, they claim; it was just 'kinds' of animal. (Whatever 'kinds' of animals means?) See eSkeptic 23 May 2007 and the article 'New creation museum opens in Kentucky' for further details of this. We would be hard pressed to contain our laughter at such naiveté were it not for the fact that these people are pushing to have this nonsense accepted as genuine history.

Irreducible complexity is another favourite con-trick of the creationists. They state that the 'perfectly formed' eye, the bacterial flagella motor or a banana (apparently) are irreducibly complex creations and could not have arisen through evolution. They are, therefore, examples of god's hand. They are not. Each evolved and this has been proven as fact. (See Dawkins' book *Climbing Mount Improbable.*) However hard they try, creationists, like the founders of the Christian church, resort to cheating and invention. There is no evidence for a deity. If there were, it would have been found by now. There would be neither doubts nor so much variation. Theists are pulling the equivalent of nylon rabbits from hats with holes over trap doors in fake tables to prove their magic works.

Philosophical atheism, with its broader strokes, casts its net further afield but takes in evidence drawn from all scientific and philosophical angles. By drawing on various disciplines an overall picture of the natural world can be built up. Is there a reason for the supernatural? (No) Wouldn't the existence of a god contradict the laws of physics? (Yes)

> By dealing with the traits that the particular, more specialized sciences have in common, the branches of philosophy serve as unifying forces, enabling man to integrate the specialized sciences within a systematic framework of knowledge.
>
> George E Smith,
> *Atheism: The Case Against God*

By comparing biology with psychology and chemistry, and so on, we build up, by degrees, the big picture of reality wherein evidence for a god is nowhere to be found. Theists use the '*design*' argument. There is order in the universe and that could only have come from god – the order implies a designer who has created it. But, as we know, order can come from disorder quite naturally – the most obvious example of this is the universe itself. (See *Not By Design* by Victor Stenger.)

The (very rarely stable) philosopher Immanuel Kant (1724–1804) was an advocate of speculative atheism. He decided that it was impossible to prove the existence of a deity. Kant has always been seen as a religious man although some have argued recently, rather convincingly, that he was, in fact, an atheist at heart. (See AC Grayling's article in *New Humanist* of July/August 2006.) He is most famous for his revolutionary *Critique of Pure Reason* in which he turned his attention to the role the mind has in constructing the outside world.

The Blindingly Obvious

Two arguments for the non-existence of a deity are linked to the fact that there are non-believers. The Buddhists and the Jains, for instance, have developed whole religions (religio-philosophies) based on non-belief and they are highly moralistic. This obviously runs counter to the theists' nonsense that we all need to bow down to the gods to be decent people.

The other is the most obvious. Why is there so much evil in the world? It is wrong to define natural disasters as evil, but this still leaves the death and destruction humanity inflicts on itself. Why the starving, the sick and homeless? Why the incessant warfare? Environmental destruction? Disease, deformity and the loss of innocent life? Why do young children die at the hands of murderers while theistic despots are allowed to run rampant, killing and maiming in the name of their god? A benevolent and omnipotent god looks on and does nothing. The inescapable conclusion is that he is, in fact, neither moral nor all-powerful – indeed the most likely and logical conclusion is that he doesn't exist. Even if he does nothing, claiming that we have freewill and that it's up to us, it is the height of immorality to do so. Where's the morality in the death of an innocent child just to teach us his love?

For further discussion of these arguments, see: *Nonbelief and Evil: Two Arguments for the Non-existence of God* by Theodore M. Drange.

Atheism and Morality

[Atheism] *equips us to face life, with its multitude*
of trials and tribulations, better than any code of
living that I have yet been able to find...
    Joseph Lewis, *Atheism and Other Addresses.*

Theists like to hold up the bible as the source of their morality.
A little investigation shows that this is not a very wise thing to
do. Most, if not all, 'holy' books are full of rape, torture, racism,
murder, misogyny and genocide and provide a *carte blanche* to
destroy unbelievers. Moses told his armies to destroy everything
and to keep captured virgins for the use thereof. Jesus (let's just
for argument's sake say he existed) seems to come across as a
racist. At one point in the gospels of both Matthew and Mark he
even refers to Gentiles as dogs. He also made it clear he didn't
care a jot for anyone who did not belong to the lost house of
Israel. Love thy neighbour? Jesus didn't. Anyone who wasn't his
follower was, in his view, going straight to hell. These are not
isolated examples. The whole bible is full of instances of very
dubious morality yet it is seen as a book that must be revered. To
many, it is inviolate. It was the screaming contradictions in the
work that led Thomas Paine to quip that the bible seemed to be
more the work of a demon than a benevolent deity, such was the
horror that occurred within its pages.

So what's the best way to define morality? Well, here's a list
of a few words that might help in defining it: sincerity, truthful-
ness, benevolence, fidelity, honesty, fairness and justice. There
are, of course, many more and not one of them requires people
to believe in some big ghost in order to achieve them. Despite
what the god-fearing claim, one can be a perfectly decent
upright and moral citizen and still be an atheist. Morality actually occurs readily throughout nature and there are numerous

examples of altruism, including reciprocal altruism, in many animal species, e.g. dolphins, elephants, meerkats and ants. Since humans are animals, it is only natural that they behave in similar fashion. Morality is hot-wired into our brains.

Atheists are decent, moral people. We do not need a despotic deity to tell us what to do or not do. Theists, on the other hand, view humanity as children that have to be threatened with a reward/punishment process in order to coerce them into right behaviour. Religious morality is nothing more than authoritarian diktat from on high. Obedience is right, disobedience wrong. Religion has been built upon the basic fear of death or rather what happens after death. The rationalist says there is no afterlife (why should there be?) while the theist says that not only is there life after death it has two levels – a heaven and a hell. Two totally abstract fantasy worlds that defy logic and reason but are there as part of the system of control through reward or punishment. This is not morality. Instilling fear in individuals, especially children, is deeply immoral – whatever excuses are mustered in its defence.

Atheism is not immoral nor does it promote immorality – being an atheist does not give non-believers carte blanche to run riot. To accuse atheism of the misperceived decline in morality is like a pyromaniac priest blaming the fire in his church on an innocent stranger who happens to be walking by. Religion is in no position to dictate to atheists about morality.

Our morality and the awareness of the plight of others; we are better now than we have ever been in terms of the awareness of human suffrage, has improved and all this in the face of religion. To claim that morality is purely a Christian creation is also false. The Greeks had developed a system of ethics before Christianity anyway as in deed had most societies.

For further discussion of these points, see *Forbidden Fruit: The*

Ethics of Humanism by Paul Kurtz; *What is Atheism? A Short Introduction* by Douglas Krueger; *The Philosophy of Humanism* by Corliss Lamont; *Ethics Without God* by Kai Nielsen; *Ethics: Discovering Right and Wrong* by Louis Pojman; *The End of Faith: Religion, Terror and the Future of Reason* by Sam Harris; *The Origins of Virtue* by Matt Ridley; *The Selfish Gene* by Richard Dawkins and *The Science of Good and Evil: Why People Cheat, Gossip, Care, Share, and Follow the Golden Rule* by Michael Shermer. *In Defence of Atheism: The Case Against Christianity, Judaism and Islam* by Michael Onfray, Robert Hinde's *Why Good is Good*, Michael Shermer's *The Science of Good and Evil*, Robert Buckman's *Can We Be Good Without God?*, and Marc Hauser's *Moral Minds*.

Are Atheists Happy?

> *Do you need a damn God and his paradise to make you happy? Can't you make your own happiness on Earth all by yourselves?*
>
> Emile Zola, *Germinal*

In a word, yes! Undoubtedly, there are many who are not. Equally there are countless theists who are miserable and depressed. How, though, do we define happiness? Anyone who is happy all the time is probably close to being a psychotic. 'Contentment' is probably a better word but, for the purposes of this argument, 'happiness' will be used.

Theists hold some pretty peculiar ideas about the mindsets of atheists and jump to some strange conclusions on the basis of their assumptions. Not the least of these is that all atheists deny their natural desire for god. As a direct consequence, frustration follows and, hot on the heels of that, misery. To theists, a godless world is necessarily an unhappy world.

All theists will state that atheism equates with unhappiness, as if the non-believer, having given up god, must have also have given up joy. The implication is that somehow belief in a supreme creator guarantees boundless and unfettered happiness. Or, even more weirdly, that contentment can only come through belief in a god. If there is no supernatural element to existence, then unhappiness must follow. This is plainly false, if not downright ridiculous, but statements of this kind are made all the time by theists. And, when all else has failed, the religious have a tendency to launch into therapy. This is why they invite people to church with the notion that their lives will be enriched, fulfilled and rewarded with boundless happiness. As if enrichment, fulfilment and happiness were entirely unavailable elsewhere.

Theists also make use of some astonishing, logic-defying twaddle to justify their position. George H Smith quotes the theologian David Trueblood in his book *Atheism: The Case Against God*, 'To be a man is to fear god. God, who is the author of nature, is integral to the nature of man. Therefore the man who does not fear god somehow does not exist, and his nature is somehow not human. On the other hand, there he is. That is the problem.' As Smith is swift to point out, Trueblood thinks that an atheist is less than human, 'to be an enigma, a walking paradox, a psychological problem'. In short, he believes that to be an atheist means that you don't exist. It is difficult to exaggerate just how silly this argument is.

In addition, atheists are often accused (falsely) of nihilism. There may well be some individual atheists who are nihilistic but that does not mean that atheism as a general philosophy is necessarily so. Some versions of Christianity, it could be argued, are themselves nihilistic. What about those sects, who teach predetermination, the belief that you're condemned to hell anyway for some idiocy called original sin? Some theists view humanity as basically unsalvageable. They prefer us to be automata without the ability to exercise our free will. How is that not nihilistic? Is the submission theists practise when they prostrate themselves before their god not nihilistic?

To denounce atheism as nihilistic is silly and untenable. Countless non-believers have contributed to the sum of human knowledge – they may well have contributed more than theists. Theists must define what exactly they mean by a purpose in life. Having children, climbing mountains, pushing back the frontiers of science, writing novels, charity work (the list is endless) – these are all purposes to life and all of them have been enjoyed by atheists. All of us can aspire to great things without believing in the gods.

Nothing to Defend

Atheism has nothing to defend. The burden of proof must rest with those who have religious beliefs and we must not accept 'faith' as an answer. It is up to them to bring forward the evidence for the existence of their deity or deities. So far, they have failed to do this. Why is a supposed universal constant, like a god, so impossible to discover?

Creationists continue to battle to inflict their views on others, resorting usually to feeble *ad hominem* attacks on those who have proved beyond doubt that the beliefs of, for instance, the so-called 'young earthers' are founded on fresh air. They can offer nothing by way of evidence to support their archaic, medieval thinking. Their most frequently used argument has been that of irreducible complexity but this is now defunct. This is the idea that a biological system, such as a wing, can have no intermediate stages or precursors, as creationists claim evolution implies. What's the use, they say, of half a wing? Dawkins and others have demolished the idiocy behind this argument. The bacterial flagella motor (a biological '*engine*') has been another frequently used example of irreducible complexity but it has turned out to be entirely inappropriate to the argument. To the likes of Michael Behe, arch creationist and author of Intelligent Design literature such as *Darwin's Black Box*, this is evidence of a creator but all biologists worth their salt have long ago burst this delusional balloon. If this is the best evidence they can put forward, then Behe and his fellow creationists have been hoisted by their own petards. (See *Climbing Mount Improbable* and *The Blind Watchmaker* by Richard Dawkins and *Why People Believe Weird Things* by Michael Shermer.)

In recent years there has been an odd alliance between Christian fundamentalists, with their bogus Intelligent Design, Neoconservatives and the Left. Evolution, science and atheism are seen to be undermining the morality of, particularly, American values. A number of intellectuals, who themselves accept evolution as true, hypocritically think that it is better for ordinary people to believe it is false. In short, what they are saying is, '*Give the peasants a sop to work with. It'll keep them quiet and subdued.*' (See Steven Pinker's *The Blank Slate: The Modern Denial of Human Nature* for a fuller exploration of this.) The Right fear atheistic revolution; the Left fear evolutionary eugenics and the destruction of certain of their political beliefs. But reality knows no political bias – it is what it is.

Atheism, it seems, has to defend itself from both ends of the political spectrum. This coalition of left and right fears that disbelief, together with evolution and science as a whole, is destroying humanity's hallowed place in the grand scheme of things. Man's privileged position in the universe was created, it should be remembered, by humanity itself through the teachings of religion.

Or, consider the odd reasoning of early twentieth century writers such as John Foster and Dr Chalmers that allowed them to label atheism as nothing short of an absurdity. They stated that, for individuals to be atheists and put forward the statement that there is no evidence for a god, they must have travelled and explored the entire universe. Atheists had no right to their beliefs until they had systematically searched for evidence of a god and found none. On closer scrutiny it is obvious that this is a ridiculous proposition, not only in the light of modern cosmology, but because theists often make the claim that god is everywhere. Surely, then, he could be found just by looking at one's feet. If the evidence is not to hand, why should it be anywhere else in the cosmos? Even in some remote corner kept well out of reach of prying eyes. The reverse argument can also be levelled at these theists. How can you know god exists everywhere without travelling the universe?

See Douglas E. Krueger's *What is Atheism? A Short Introduction*, Richard Dawkin's *The God Delusion*, Victor Stenger's *God: The Failed Hypothesis*, George E. Smith's *Atheism: The Case Against God* and Christopher Hitchens' *God is Not Great: How Religion Poisons Everything*.

Atheism – A Brief History

Disbelief crept over me at a very slow rate,
but at last it was complete.

Charles Darwin,
Autobiography

It is recommended that readers acquaint themselves with Jonathan Miller's excellent television programme *A History of Disbelief*, and with the books, *What is Good?* by AC Grayling; *2000 Years of Disbelief: Famous People with the Courage to Doubt* by James Haught; *A Short History of Western Atheism* by James Thrower.

Now it is time for a quick, whistle-stop tour through the history of atheism.

Atheism: The Early Years

Religion comes from the period of human prehistory where
nobody had the smallest idea what was going on.

Christopher Hitchens, *God is not Great:*
How Religion Poisons Everything.

We find it in ancient Egypt in spite of the scantiness of the literary remains and the despotic power of the priests. We see it so widespread in civilization 2,500 years ago that it takes a prominent place in history in the form of the Ionian philosophy of Greece and the ethic of Buddha and Confucius in Asia.

*Then there is the high cultural development of the Greek-Roman civiliza-
tion, and from 300 BC to 300 AD we find the thinly veiled Atheism of the
Stoics, Epicureans, and Sceptics accepted by the great majority of the better
educated. Atheism perishes again with the crass ignorance and clerical
tyranny of the Iron Age, but it spreads widely in the light of the Arab-Persian
civilization, wherever the fanatics are checked, and at the Renaissance it
reappears in Christendom. The hardening of the religious attitude after the
Reformation again checks it, but in the 18th Century it enters upon a development, which has, in spite of murderous clerical tyranny in some countries,
proceeded steadily ever since.*

Joseph McCabe
Rise and Fall of the Gods (1931)

Just how far atheism goes back in time can never really be ascer-
tained and its true position in the ancient world can only be
described as uncertain at best. Although it may seem unlikely,
there may very well have been non-believers in some of the
earliest religions known to the human species. Perhaps, these
early religions were, in effect, survival systems based on the
observations and worship of sun, moon and the stars – the celestial gods. Perhaps, they were used as aids to migration. 'When
the sun is this high in the sky, we move to the warmer climes in
the south.' In other words, early religion was the worship of
astronomy – the remnants of which, via Egyptian religion – Ra,
via the Greeks – Helios, and the Romans – Apollo, have
continued all the way up to the present day and are seen as the
inner symbolism of all faiths e.g. the crescent moon of Islam or
the halo of Christianity – stolen from the *Sol Invictus* cult. To
deny the existence of something readily visible in the day or
night sky would have seemed distinctly odd. Who could deny the
existence of the sun? One did not need 'faith' to see the moon.
Faith, as we understand it, though, the ephemeral mainstay of
religion, may not have been part of the equation.

Into this would have been mixed story telling, myth building, shamanism, totemism, fetishism, tribal bonding and ancestor worship, all attempts at describing and illustrating that sense of the numinous which perhaps developed only when our species had more time on its hands. In the life-and-death situations encountered by early hominids there would have been no need for religion, which would have wasted valuable mental processing. In Darwinian terms, it may well not have existed, developing only as a corruption of an inbuilt neurological survival mechanism — a hunting rite of protection, for example. By taking on its spirit in a ceremony of sympathetic magic — a form of possession — the hunter might very well have thought he was more likely to catch his prey.

Religion may also have had its roots in the expansion of consciousness — an offshoot of the awareness of mind. In tribal terms it may well have existed as a bond against the enemy — a social glue to unite individuals into a common cause. Dissent (or disbelief) in such circumstances would have meant disaster — the destruction of the group identity. Even today, armies in times of conflict are bonded through training and the idealistic notion they are fighting for, say, 'queen and country' or for 'liberty' and/or 'freedom'. Early societies may have benefited from this kind of social, cohesion rooted in religion.

With the coming of agriculture and the fall of the nomadic lifestyle, religions would have developed into variations of this celestial worship. Seasonal observations of astronomical and meteorological phenomena for crop planting and the enhance-ment and binding of community would have been added to the mix. Animism — the worships of spirits or *numina* (in Roman culture) that existed in trees, water, springs, the home — would have been a strong presence. There was also the sexual element in religious practices — for example, the use of the phallus in Egyptian worship and in many creation myths. In fact, early religion could well be described as nothing more than the symbolism of sex and astronomy.

Ritual may have developed from the misperceived outcomes of certain actions and unrelated phenomena. Flipping a stone in a pool of water coincided with the appearance of deer – a meal. The hunter would then repeat the actions in the hope of a similar outcome. The location of this coincidence may eventually have become hallowed ground for the hunter and his tribe and a basic religion would have grown up around that site. The ancient Gauls, for example, thought the sky was forever in danger of falling on their heads and they worshipped various gods, such as Toutatis, to stop that happening. (Had they observed natural phenomena like meteorites and come to the wrong conclusion?) As the sky had not yet fallen, praying to the gods obviously worked. There was further reinforcement to continuing belief in the power of Toutatis and his fellow gods.

When people had time to think, then they had time to discuss religious beliefs and maybe it was only then that the seeds of doubt began to germinate. But relinquishing rituals – supposedly formulae for survival – may well have been simply too much. Life was nasty, brutish and short and fear, as it is today, was part and parcel of religion. To cease to perform magic ceremonies might have resulted in disaster. We now know that the magic didn't work but, to early men, the world was a much harsher place than today and one filled with great unknowns. Why give up something that appeared to work?

Religious experience may also have come about through the ingestion of toxins, hallucinogens and decaying food. An individual consumes poisonous berries or a mushroom and then describes the mystical experience he or she had. This 'experience' then enters the mindset of the tribe – a meme is born. Memes, a concept devised by Richard Dawkins, are elements of culture that can be passed from mind to mind. They can comprise a wide variety of cultural phenomena, from a tune to the idea of rubbing sticks together to create fire.

Alternatively, it may very well be that religion works only to develop itself as a meme-plex – a virus of the mind. As Dawkins writes in *The God Delusion*:

> *The fact that religion is ubiquitous probably means that it has worked for the benefit of something, but it may not be us or our genes. It may be to the benefit of only the religious ideas themselves, to the extent that they behave in a somewhat gene-like way, as replicators.*

In other words 'religion' is looking out for itself. Religion is nothing more than a mental parasite. (See also Dawkins' book *The Selfish Gene* and Susan Blackmore's *The Meme Machine* for a detailed description of memes and meme-plexes.)

Atheism goes hand in hand with scepticism and advancing knowledge and the assumption might be that, due to a lack of understanding of how the real world worked, it would have been difficult for it to develop in prehistory. However, it is more likely that, without a dominating established '*church*', atheism would have had full rein to thrive. There was no one great institution able to dictate methods of thought and to bully disbelievers. Dissent would have been more prevalent.

What is very clear though is that, for millennia prior to Christianity, humanity did just fine. All this unnecessary talk of messiahs being sent to save us was, and still is, patronising. We don't need saving, then or now. It is interesting to speculate how much more advanced we would have been had we not had to deal with the anti-intellectualism of the major faiths that have developed in the last 1,700 years or so. They have done nothing but halt the progress of our species and a great deal of effort has been wasted in countering their claims.

See – *The Psychology of Religious Behaviour, Belief and Experience* by Benjamin Beit-Hallahmi and M. Argyle, *Religion Explained* by P. Boyer; *Breaking the Spell: Religion as a Natural Phenomenon* by Daniel Dennett and *How We Believe: The Search for God in the Age of Science* by Michael Shermer.

The Egyptians

There is no strong evidence for atheism in Egyptian belief. The Greek historian Herodotus described the Egyptians as being the most religious of peoples, which would suggest that it was unlikely atheism found a foothold in their society. Perhaps this is a sweeping statement, for who can say that everyone followed devoutly the faiths built up around deities such as Ra, Amun, Osiris and Isis? Who can say for certain that disbelief was not present? Feasts were accompanied by harpists who encouraged the revellers to have a good time because life after death was not a given. They also stated that no one ever came back from the dead to tell the living about immortality. Perhaps modern TV mediums should take note. (See *A Companion to Ethics*, edited by Peter Singer.)

India

The first stirrings of genuine atheism are to be found in India. The Hindu scriptures, the Vedas, written in Sanskrit and dating as far back as 4000 BPE, were to inspire Buddhism, Jainism and the *Sankhaya* sect of Hinduism. Buddhism was started some 2,500 years BPE by Gautama Siddhartha, the first Buddha or enlightened one. Although it has no gods, Buddhism does believe in a supernatural force called karma and, like all religions, it uses reward and condemnation as a system of control. Right action is rewarded by the ultimate goal of *nirvana*, 'blowing out', the extinction of self, while wrong action is punished by reincarnation into a multitude of lives or *samsara*, a continual round of suffering much akin to the Christian hell. Buddhism can be criticised for its claims that individuals who are suffering in this life are doing so because of something they did in their past lives. Despite Buddhism's appearance of being a 'good' religion, this is nothing more than social and moral indifference. It is morally offensive to suggest a child is born handicapped because of supposed wrongdoing in a previous life.

Jainism, one of the influences on Gandhi, was an offshoot of Hinduism and began around the same time as Buddhism. It was born from the teachings of Mahavira, the last of a line of 24 masters. Jainism, with its two distinct divisions (the *Digambaras* and the *Swetambaras*), has no gods but believes, like Buddhism, in karma. The basic tenet is that no harm should be done to any living thing and the Jainist code of ethics is based on compassion for all life. In essence, Jainism is an atheistic religion yet, with its respect for all life, it practises a highly advanced morality. Its very existence counters beautifully the nonsensical claims that a god must be present for morality to flourish and it developed centuries before Christianity or Islam appeared.

Sankhaya, sometimes *sankhya*, was another offshoot of Hinduism. Again it has no god. The *Sankhya-sutras*, ascribed to Kapila, are often described as the realistic school of orthodox Indian philosophy. It is one of the six main divisions of its mother religion and its teachings are about the eternal interaction between matter and spirit. It states that the universe has developed through unconscious evolution rather than through the actions of a deity.

Despite their atheistic tendencies, the Hinduistic offshoots of

Buddhism, Jainism and Sankhaya were still steeped in their heritage and possessed many supernatural elements but at least they were taking steps in the right direction.

Materialism

Over in the Mediterranean, some centuries later, the Greeks were starting to develop ideas centred on materialism. Their version of materialism stated that there was nothing in existence other than matter and matter in motion. Some of its tenets were similar to those of early Buddhism but it denied the supernatural. In other words, the Greek materialists were atheists. (Their kind of materialism should not be confused with the modern materialism, which centres on the desire for a new fridge or computer.) Archimedes (287–212 BC) was the first to say that physics drove the universe not the gods. The sun rises because of natural laws not by prayer.

Greek philosophy, as a whole, was an attempt to understand and therefore to teach the best ways to live, through wisdom and the holding of the right opinions about the gods, man, the world and virtue. In short, it combined religion, metaphysics and morals. There were a number of schools that developed these ideas, the first being that of Miletus founded by Thales. In these various schools, the great names of Greek philosophy espoused their various ideas about the universe.

The first to formulate ideas of materialism were Leucippus (5th century BC) and Democritus (460–370 BC) who both described the universe as made up of atoms. This atomic theory became the basis for the ethics of the Epicureans and later for many Romans. The Roman poet Lucretius in his work *De Rerum Natura* particularly shows the influence of the theory on later writers and thinkers.

Leucippus, of whom very little is known, emerged from the third school of Elea, founded by Parmenides and carried on by Zeno. This school made the distinction between the single eternal and unchangeable reality and the unreal phenomena of change and motion. Other philosophers associated with the school included Anaxagoras, born around 500 BC, who was the first man to explain solar eclipses and suffer banishment because he said the sun was a white hot stone, and Empedocles (490 – 430 BC) who committed suicide by hurling himself into Mt Etna. Leucippus, in a step of brilliant reasoning, decided that matter was made up of plural not single constituents and thus became the originator of the atomistic philosophy, which stated that the universe is made up of a vast number of atoms that combine to form matter mechanically i.e. without divine help.

The well-travelled Democritus, sometimes known as the 'laughing philosopher', also wrote works, praised by the likes of Cicero and Plutarch, on music, natural philosophy, mathematics and morals. He stated that atoms make up matter but, when the various forms this takes collapse and decay, the atoms themselves remain intact. This was yet another superb insight for the time. Admittedly, Democritus also believed the soul was a subtle form of fire that animated the human body and that to gain happiness one must recognise the superiority it had over the body, but at least he said that it too was made from atoms and was not something ethereal and insubstantial. When its owner died, the soul died too.

The Greeks were pushing the gods further into the shadows while thinkers like Aristotle promoted 'aretaic' ethics, which concentrated on the character of the individual as opposed to the rightness and wrongness of an action. The debate was not about what was right and wrong per se but about what kind of life to lead. If society could promote right conduct in individuals there would be no need to worry.

Then came Epicurus (341–270 BC) who, like the above-mentioned philosophers, was a materialist. Born in Samos, he founded the Epicurean School in Athens. It was known as *Ho Kepos* ('the Gardens') because Epicurus liked to teach al fresco. His teachings were collected together in the *Sovran Maxims*, the top forty of his ideas, which included his fundamental notion that the right way to live should be drawn from reliance on the senses and from the elimination of superstition, belief in an afterlife and the idiotic notion that life was under divine control. He accepted Democritus' atomic theory and stated that every event had a natural cause. According to Cicero, the Romans took to Epicureanism with gusto. Like some classical Banksy, Diogenes Laertius (200–250 AD), in a delightful display of intellectual vandalism, even carved the man's teachings on to a portico wall.

Epicurus is more famous for his ethics, which, in later years, were horribly misinterpreted by theists to suggest that the philosopher believed solely in the kind of hedonism that involves lounging around and eating grapes. In fact, he stated that pleasure, the absence of pain, is the only good, being the only good known to the senses, and that the best pleasure, with no painful want, is a perfect harmony of mind and body. This was to be sought not in hedonism but in simple virtuous living.

The Epicurean doctrine can be summed up as: 'Nothing to fear in god. Nothing to feel in death. Good can be attained. Evil can be endured.' Various schools teaching this survived until the fourth century AD. He was influential over such major Latin writers as Horace, Virgil and Marcus Aurelius.

The Cynics

As AC Grayling describes them, the Cynics were, 'in essence, hippies, drop-outs, anti-establishment figures'. Their basic idea was that the world was such a cesspool of corruption, death and destruction, that Fortune, randomly in control of events, was the only 'divine' presence. If you get a cheque in the post, you're just as likely to be shot dead by a stray arrow on the way to the bank. Diogenes of Sinope (not to be confused with Diogenes Laertius) flourished in the fourth Century BC and was known as the 'Heavenly Dog'. The son of a banker, he taught that the best way to live your life was simply and in harmony with nature. In many respects the philosophy of the Cynics also resembled Buddhism in its rejection of futile desires, wants and needs. Like Buddhism, it also taught that all the nonsense in life was the result of people's greed and ambition. But, unlike Buddhism, it involved no need for a lengthy intellectual journey of deep thought. Enlightenment was to be found through living with a direct link to one's instincts, desires and impulses – which included, in Diogenes' case, masturbating in public and weeing up a tree in a restaurant (thus predating the English lager lout abroad by some two thousand years).

Diogenes' attack on religion was prompted by what he thought was its control over people's lives – it enslaved them while promoting a fear of death. He had no time for priests, superstitions, soothsayers or the entire bogus scam that was the supernatural. Dressed only in a cloak, he would wander the streets, shaking his fist and shouting at anyone he thought worthy of a verbal dressing down or, as legend has it, taking up residence in an earthenware tub in the *Metroum*, the Sanctuary of the Mother of the Gods at Athens. Visitors often travelled from afar to be abused by a man living in a pot.

The Stoics

The Stoics were founded in Athens in 315 BC by one Zeno of Citium. The name Stoic comes from the *Stoa Poilike*, the porch of paintings created by the mural artist Polygnotus (475 – 445 BC) where Zeno held court. In sharp contrast to Epicurus, Zeno thought the world to be a rational, organic whole, controlled by the four elements and by *logos* – reason. Logos held the four elements in tension and it was variously seen as the 'soul of the world', the 'fire of the world', or Zeus. But Stoics did not believe in a separate god per se. The universe was seen to be in a perpetual cycle of death, journeying into the divine fire and then into rebirth into a likeness of its predecessor. The theory has similarities to what is known as the '*Brahmin Year*' in Hinduism or to the modern cosmological idea in which Big Bang is followed by Big Crunch and then once more by Big Bang.

This driving force in Stoicism was an organisational one – for the soul of the universe in the same way as for the soul of a man. Into this basic belief were blended the teachings of Heraclitus, who said that reason was the creative principle and that the universe was in a constant state of change, and the teachings of Socrates who believed in the search for truth through rationality and self mastery. The Stoics thought that all men, whoever they were, should be treated with respect as all represented the divine spark. Their philosophy was about benevolence and justice and the search for virtue and harmony. The Epicureans thought possessions to be a hindrance but the Stoics came to realise that owning certain things was actually a benefit. Epicurus said that the inbuilt drive was for pleasure whereas the Stoics thought it was one for self-preservation in which pain was accepted as part of the growing process. In short, they were, in the broadest of terms, humanists. Stoicism was to prove a major influence on the Romans.

The Sceptics

Scepticism, in the Greek tradition, was a school of philosophy founded by Pyrrhon (365–275 BC). Pyrrhon decided that evidence derived from the senses and the way the mind worked was so contradictory that it negated any certainty about the workings of reality. Knowledge about the nature of the world was ultimately unobtainable. Scepticism, at its heart, involved nothing more than a suspension of judgement coupled with mental quietude and indifference to the activities of the outside world. Again, there are similarities to aspects of Buddhism. For Stoics, the gods must be dismissed because there was no evidence for them. Nothing can be known for certain since humanity lacks the means to discover the true nature of the world.

In modern times, the word 'scepticism' has taken on a more pejorative meaning in that it is seen as an illiberal rejection, by sour-faced scientists, of everything. But it isn't. Its roots are in the Greek word meaning 'thoughtful' – scepticism demands that one must keep an open mind or, rather, not accept everything at face value. Carl Sagan highlighted this in his lecture entitled 'Burden of Scepticism' by saying:

> It seems to me what is called for is an exquisite
> balance between two conflicting needs: the most sceptical
> scrutiny of all hypotheses that are served up to us and at
> the same time a great openness to new ideas. If you are
> only sceptical then no new ideas make it through to you.
> You never learn anything new. You become a crotchety
> old person convinced that nonsense is ruling the world
> (There is much evidence to support you.) On the other
> hand, if you are open to the point of gullibility and have
> not an ounce of sceptical sense in you, then you cannot
> distinguish useful ideas from the worthless ones. If all

ideas have equal validity then you are lost, because then,
it seems to me, no ideas have any validity at all.

Of course, the Sceptics could not know the great strides that science would make in future centuries. Scientific and technological advances have given us certainties about the real world, which the ancient Sceptics had decided was unknowable.

The outlook of modern sceptics can be best expressed by quoting Spinoza who said, 'I have made a ceaseless effort not to ridicule, not to bewail, not to scorn human actions, but to understand them.'

See also www.skeptic.com

Euhemerism

Euhemerus (3rd century BC) was a Sicilian Greek who wrote the *Hiera Anagraphe*, an imaginary history of an island called Panchaea, supposedly located in the Indian Ocean. The central idea of the book was that the gods of mythology had their origins in the activities of mortal kings and heroes who were then subsequently deified by the people over whom they had once had control, either dictatorial or benign. These ideas influenced Ennius, one of the early Roman poets.

Lucretius

Nature free at once and rid of her haughty lords
is seen to do all things spontaneously of herself
without the meddling of the gods...
Lucretius, *De Rerum Natura*

Lucretius (99–55 BC), one of the greatest Roman poets and

philosophers, came to prominence at a time when the old religions were losing ground within the educated classes and a general sense of scepticism prevailed. At this time, superstition was rife and Lucretius remarks that, adopting a kind of 'just in case' mentality, even those who profess to despise the gods still make sacrifices to them.

Lucretius' life remains largely a mystery and even St Jerome's biography of him is full of uncertainty but it is clear that he was a man of scientific inquiry with a sharp mind. He is best known for the gloriously atheistic work, *De Rerum Natura* ('*On the Nature of Things*'), and he was a strict Epicurean. His most famous work, six books written in hexameters, sets out to dispel superstitions and to describe the movement of atoms through their own volition and their coming together to create mass – the material things of which the universe is made. There is no room for the gods in this, although Lucretius accepted that they existed. However, they did not create the world and played no part in the affairs of men. He then went on to admonish religion for its promotion of terror and fear. He derided the Stoics and had a pop or two at the Platonists and the Pythagoreans for their reliance on gods and their teaching of soul survival after death – an idea that was later to influence Christianity. Although he believed in a soul, he said that it dies with the mortal body. He was probably the most famous proto-atheist of his age. His work and influence is mentioned in the *Georgics*, the agricultural poems of Virgil. It is claimed that he drank a love potion, administered by his wife, which sent him insane and led eventually to his taking of his own life. It is impossible to know whether or not this is true but the story smacks of character assassination – an embodiment of the idea that rejection of the gods necessarily sends one mad.

The Late Classical Era and the Dark Ages

After the cult of Christianity began to flourish, there was a last great surge of old-school classicism, predominantly in the form of Neoplatonism. The chief exponents of this school were Plotinus, Porphyry and the famous Hypatia, daughter of the mathematician Theon, who was murdered by Alexandrian Christians in 415 AD. The last great name in Neoplatonist thought was that of Proclus of Byzantium whose writings strongly supported the paganism that was rapidly falling prey to advancing Christianity.

The West soon fell into the dark ages and, while the fathers of the new church were busy cobbling together their religion, forging documents and the existence of a messiah, freethinking fell into the backseat. Undoubtedly, there were those who questioned belief, both in the Christian tradition and in the still extant pagan religions, but they never bothered writing anything down. They may well have been too busy fleeing their persecutors.

During the ninth century it must have seemed, to the population of the newly emerging England, that the new religion had something to it. In 878, after the Peace of Wedmore, King Alfred converted Guthrum, leader of the Viking hordes, to Christianity. Guthrum was baptized at Aller in Somerset and given the new name Athelstan. Alfred stood as godfather. Christianity, it seemed, had conquered the pagans. Alfred used the faith to solidify his power and unite a country. Subsequently, atheism took a back seat for a long time.

The Middle Ages

If there were any atheists at this time, they failed to make their ideas known. During the centuries of the Middle Ages, superstition and religious zeal were at their height, as Christianity ruled the roost throughout Europe. In such surroundings, atheists would not have lasted long anyway. Some Marxist philosophers have argued that the roots of atheism or, rather, of the continuing fermentation of atheistic thought were to be found within the various heresies of the time. The idea is debatable but worth consideration. In Asia, meanwhile, Buddhism and Jainism, both religions with a 'no gods' policy, continued to thrive.

The Renaissance

The great flourishing of art, learning and the revival of pagan classicism known as the Renaissance was the next great experiment in free thought, blending Epicureanism, the syncretism of the Stoics and the Neoplatonists and the view that the world was self-contained and self-sufficient. It began in Italy in the fourteenth century and lasted until the end of the sixteenth century. Elsewhere in Europe it went on for another hundred years or so. In brief, the Renaissance represented a shift from a contemplative life to one of active exploration of the world and the individual's place in it. It embraced humanism, the basis for atheism, and the republican ideal. Much of this was born on the back of the re-discovery of ancient, classical texts that had been kept safe for centuries in the Arab world.

Of course, to counter this, the Inquisition had great fun throwing freethinkers to the flames at countless 'bring a heretic' parties that were all the rage at the time. The church, flushed purple with apoplexy, attempted to clamp down on all this radicalism. At the same time, some of the greatest minds in history were flexing their mental muscles. These included the genius and polymath Leonardo da Vinci (1452–1519); Galileo Galilei (1564–1642), the famous astronomer, and inventor of the telescope, who was told to give up silly ideas of the sun being the orbital centre of the solar system by the Inquisition, the Pope's Gestapo; Johannes Kepler (1571–1630), another mathematician, astronomer and optics expert, Desiderius Erasmus (1466–1536), humanist and religion-basher, and the most famous atheist of the time, Giordano Bruno (1548–1600), who was burnt at the stake for his troubles. He had written a book entitled *De La Causa, Principio Et Uno* in which he said that god had no place in an infinite universe.

Humanism also developed during these years and was best embodied by Dutchman Desiderius Erasmus (1466–1536) who exemplified the all-round educated individual well-versed in the arts. He wrote the international bestseller *Encomium Moriae* ('*The Praise of Folly*'), a satire on church and society, in 1511. The ideas for humanism were based on the work of such scholars as the Italian Petrarch (1304–1374), which gained great momentum from the rediscovery of the ancient texts of the classical world.

Thomas Hobbes (1588–1679) was the first since the time of Aristotle to develop an overriding theory of nature and human existence. He rightly condemned religion as little more than nonsense. Like Raleigh and Marlowe before him, he was accused of atheism. He is best known for the idea of the 'Social Contract' – the theory expounded in his famous 1651 book, *Leviathan*, that government authority derives from an agreement between the ruler and the ruled.

Baruch Spinoza (1632–1677), a lens grinder by trade, influenced by the classicists and by the French philosopher Descartes, believed in rational pantheism, an idea frowned on by Christians because it suggested the divine was everywhere and in all things rather than in a god in some exalted position above the affairs of mortal man. Spinoza was a determinist and believed that human

affairs were motivated by an overwhelming sense of self-preservation. His only book published in his lifetime was *A Treatise on
Religious and Political Philosophy,* which appeared in the 1670s.
Christians hated it, as did his fellow Jews who ousted him from
their community for heresy. Later pantheists were Hegel (1770–
1831), JG Fichte (1762–1814) and Schelling (1775–1854).
Fichte countered Kant's idea of the 'thing in itself' in his *Critique
of Religious Revelation* of 1792 and saw 'god' as the simple active
moral order of the world. In another fine example of theistic
tolerance, he was swiftly accused of atheism and booted out of
the University of Jena.

The Age of Enlightenment

*The cause and explanation of what you do not understand may perhaps be
the simplest thing in the world. Perfect your physics and you will understand
Nature better, refine your reason, banish your prejudices and you'll have no
further need of your god.*

Marquis De Sade, *Dialogue Between a
Priest and a Dying Man*, 1782

This is the period when the fun really began and atheism really
started to find its feet. The Enlightenment was a European intellectual movement that reached its zenith in the eighteenth
century and developed from British Deism, Cartesian mechanism and empiricism. It was a period when social progress and
the development of scientific and rational thought moved to set
people free from irrational beliefs, religion and monarchy (the
ancien regime, the 'old order') which were seen as repressive
forces in the development of humanity. Newtonian physics also
played a part in this burgeoning movement as it encouraged a
rationalist way to examine the world. (See John Gribbin's
Science: A History.) The American and French Revolutions, of

1775–1783 and 1789–1799 respectively, were a direct result of a move towards basic human rights of liberty and intellectual freedom. Even in the present day, theists denounce the Enlightenment and claim that immorality has been its direct result. In fact, the opposite is true.

The proto-humanism of the Renaissance began to develop into something like full-blown atheism in the sixteenth and seventeenth centuries. Martin Luther's ranting threatened to crack Christianity and the Protestant Reformation he initiated made sure that the bible was readily available for anyone to look at. It was translated from Latin into the vernacular, allowing the peasants to read, for the first time, about the absurdities it contained. The Catholic Church was enraged by this since it removed power from the hands of the priests. They could no longer get away with peddling their lies. People could now start to ask questions. Important questions, which would, of course, cause trouble. Deism could also take a foothold and the ridiculous god of the Old Testament could be converted into something more fluffy and user-friendly. In other words, god's back-story and character were re-written. Nevertheless, the deists did want to change things and for the better. Englishman and deist John Toland (1670–1722) wrote *Christianity Not Mysterious,* which stuck the boot firmly into Christianity. For his efforts, he was hauled before the authorities and narrowly escaped accusations of blasphemy.

The period is famed for producing some of the most famous names in freethinking, including Frenchman Rene Descartes (1595–1650) of 'I think therefore I am' fame. Descartes had religious leanings, believing strongly in the soul or the *res cogitans* ('the thinking thing') and so cannot be considered an atheist. None the less, he was still able to develop his ideas of atoms, which he named 'corpuscles', together with other ideas about the natural world, which helped to influence atheism. His theory that there was a distinct realm of matter and another of mind is now known as Cartesian dualism. He was another polymath and wrote a number of books including *La Géométrié* ('Geometry') in 1637 and *Discourse on Method* in the same year.

Julien Offray De LaMettrie (1709–1751), French philosopher and physician, was born in St Malo. He studied theology then gave that up for medicine. His first book *L'Histoire Naturelle de l'Ame* ('Natural History of the Soul') of 1745 kicked up such a stink that it was publicly burnt and he had to flee to Holland. The basic tenet of this work was that psychical phenomena could be explained as nothing more than brain chemistry. He developed this idea in *L'Homme Machine* ('The Man Machine') in 1747 and once more had to leg it out of the country, this time to the protection of Frederick II of Prussia who later wrote a biography of LaMettrie after the young man's death from food poisoning. He wrote several more works including the *L'Art de Jouir* ('The Art of Enjoyment') of 1751, which proposed a modernised version of Epicureanism and other classical ideas. He argued that the only real pleasures in life are those of the senses, that virtue was enlightened self-interest and that the soul dies with the body.

One of the great focal points for thought in this period was the secular *Encyclopédie,* which was assembled by the Encyclopaedists, a group of deists and atheists. The *grande fromage* of the movement was Denis Diderot (1713–1784) who, like Voltaire and the Marquis De Sade, was imprisoned for writing books with atheistic themes. Diderot was assisted by Paris foundling Jean D'Alembert (1717–1783), the mathematician and theoretical physicist who, amongst other work, enlarged upon Newton's Third Law. He contributed many scientific writings to the *Encyclopédie*.

Paul Henri Thiry, Baron d'Holbach (1723–1789), writer of

Christianisme Dévoilé, ('Christianity Unveiled') and *The Holy Disease*, pre-empted a great many theistic critics of the French Revolution, including those today who see it purely as an atheistic uprising.

He wrote:

> *If the ministers of the Church have often permitted nations to revolt for Heaven's cause, they never allowed them to revolt against real evils or known violences. It is from Heaven that the chains have come to fetter the minds of mortals.*

He is famed for his unflinching attacks on religion, especially in his *Natural Politics*. In this, he writes that religion, by teaching people to fear supernatural dictators, allows them to fear earthly ones as well.

D'Holbach often entertained with lavish dinner evenings at his house in Paris in rue Royale, butte Saint-Roche. He had been left a vast fortune by his uncle and father in law, but these gatherings were less about the tuck and more about the intellectual discourse. The inner circle, the majority of whom were atheists, included Denis Diderot (encyclopedist), Augustin Roux (doctor), Jacques-André Naigeon (philosopher), abbé Guillame-Thomas-François Raynal (priest), Charles-Georges Le Roy (naturalist), Friedrich-Melchior Grimm (diplomat), Jean-François Marmontel (writer and critic) and abbé André Morellet (pamphleteer). D'Holbach's definition of an atheist is still worth consideration:

> [An atheist] *is a man who destroys the dreams and chimerical beings that are dangerous to the human race so that men can be brought back to nature, to experience and to reason.*

See also Alan Kors *D'Holbach's Coterie* (Princeton University Press 1976).

Another famous freethinker of the time was Thomas Paine (1737–1809). Despite his belief in a prime mover (in other words, his deism) Paine's writings would heavily influence atheists right up to the present day. He was born in Thetford in Norfolk but moved to the United States in 1774 where he became friends with Benjamin Franklin, scientist and Freemason. Paine played a major role in both the French and the American Revolutions and fought on the side of the colonists in the States. He was anti-slavery, anti-monarchist and a proto-feminist, which explains the antagonism towards him from patriarchal men of the cloth. He wrote three highly influential and famous pamphlets, *Common Sense* (1776) – which fuelled the revolutionary spark in America – *The Rights of Man* (1791) and *The Age of Reason* (1793). *The Rights of Man* was a response to Burke's right-wing *Reflections on the Revolution in France*. Paine had returned to Blighty in 1787 but was branded a traitor in 1792 so he nipped across the channel to France. There he sought political office, which he gained after dodging the guillotine and the fall of Robespierre. In 1802 he returned to the States.

Meanwhile in Germany, the German Enlightenment was in full swing and the most famous name attached to that was Immanuel Kant (1724–1804) who wrote *Die Religion Innerhalb Der Grenzen Der Blossen Vernunft* ('Religion Within the Limits of Reason Alone') in 1793. He later had to defend this in 1798, the same year that saw the beginnings of the so-called *Atheismusstreit*, or 'conflict over atheism', in which numerous theologians attempted to demolish the position of non-belief. Kant thought that the existence of god could not be proved theoretically and was one of the first to consider the mind's role in quantifying the objective world. He also wrote that ethical right action must be based on reason and not on feelings.

One of the great philosophical ideas of the period was Utilitarianism; a term coined by the great liberal defender John Stuart Mill (1806 –73). However, it was Jeremy Bentham (1748 –1836), philosopher and social reformer and the actual founder of this school of moral philosophy, who first developed the ethical doctrine that actions are morally right in proportion to their usefulness or their promotion of happiness. If an action promotes a bad outcome then it is morally wrong. Bentham actually used the term 'Utility' to describe his idea and wrote it all up in *Principles of Morals and Legislation* (written in 1780, published in 1789). In developing his ideas, he was ably assisted by John Stuart Mill's father, the Scotsman James Mill (1773–1836). Importantly, they left out any idea of god.

The overriding goal of Utilitarianism was the greatest happiness of the greatest number. The happiness of man came to be seen as the only measure of right and wrong. It was a variation of 'consequentialism' – in which the morality of an action was judged by it consequences. Bentham contributed to reforms of the Poor Law as well as proposing annual elections, the use of secret ballots and male suffrage in his work *Catechism of Parliamentary Reform* of 1817. He can still be seen in the hallway of University College London.

As AC Grayling writes in *What Is Good?*, the religious aspect of the Enlightenment was just the starting point.

> ...*the hegemony of religion over thought is, although central, not the sole concern, but just the starting point for what really counts: the project, to be undertaken by each individual, of relying on reason and applying the lessons of science as the chief guides to building better lives and societies.*

The Enlightenment has and continues to have its critics who blame it for all kinds of things from dewy-eyed utopianism to the conflicts of the twentieth century but this is to do it severe injustice. As Peter Gay makes clear in *The Enlightenment: An Interpretation*, the search for the right way to live – the good – has always come up against theistic resistance. Theologians and Christian apologists will always denounce the Enlightenment simply because it was the first great threat to their supernatural autocracy and because it was a vigorous attempt to give the church a well-deserved bloody nose. In this, it succeeded. Contrary to theistic carping The Enlightenment was certainly not responsible for fascism as some claim. The Enlightenment has nothing to do with fascism or communism — it was about liberty from religious superstition.

See Peter Gay's *The Enlightenment: An Interpretation*.

The Nineteenth Century

As the dust was settling after the French Revolution, theists rallied to resist the ungodly ways of freethinkers and blamed them for all the unrest. But, having had their 'god' exposed as a tyrannical despot, they rewrote the character to make him more loving and caring. Like a political party recreating itself on the back of a heavy defeat, Christianity attempted a re-brand. Their god had to evolve to survive. But, thankfully, the atheist genie was out of the bottle and the fractures in theology were too deep to repair. Freethought could now find its own way and the paths of religion and science were starting to diverge. Of course the French revolution was reviled by other European countries because of its potential threat to neighbouring monarchies – a touch of, '*Hang on, the peasants are revolting! They'll be wanting their basic human rights next.*'

Auguste Comte (1798–1857) founded '*Positivism*' which stated that only science and observation could produce knowledge and therefore religion and metaphysics, which lay beyond any rational empiricism, were to be rejected. By default, they were to be seen as essentially useless. On the basis of positivism Comte constructed his 'Religion of Humanity'. (Much later, in the 1920s, 'logical positivism' was developed and expounded by such thinkers as AJ Ayer and Bertrand Russell.) In his *Cours de Philosophie Positive* of 1830–42, he argued that society moves through three stages in its development – theological, metaphysical and then '*positive*' or scientific. (Theists want the reverse to happen.) He also coined the term 'sociology' in 1830.

Ludwig Andreas Feuerbach (1804–1872) had studied theology for two years but had swiftly abandoned it after the philosopher Hegel encouraged him to move to Berlin. He wrote *The Essence of Christianity* in 1841, the essence of which was that god is simply a projection of man. He started with the Hegelian idea that the Absolute comes to consciousness only in humanity and denies the idea of god having any existence beyond said human consciousness. God is simply man's projection of his ideal upon the world and nothing more. Anthropomorphism writ large.

However, while atheists and deists were busy exercising their freedom of thought and expanding their minds, illiberal theists, still dreaming of the past, maintained an upper hand. They took to using the blasphemy laws and, in 1842, the Englishman who invented the term 'secular', George Jacob Holyoake (1817–1906), was arrested for daring to say something naughty about god in a journal. Holyoake had started his working life as tinsmith but, in 1840, after a period as a Chartist and an Owenite, he became a rationalist and edited a journal called the *Oracle of Reason* in which the article that brought about his six-month prison sentence for blasphemy appeared. He later edited other journals — *The Reasoner* (1846), *The Leader* (1850) and, finally, *The Secular Review* in 1876. Holyoake was an advocate of free thought and electoral reform.

Theists thought that they could, at best, contain the godless freethinkers and keep them in check but their hopes of returning god to an exalted position were soon to be dashed. There was trouble just up ahead, trouble that would take everyone, including the scientific world, by surprise. In 1859, Charles Darwin published what is, it is correct to say, the most important book in the history of humanity. It was *The Origin of Species*, a work that explained the world in realistic terms and as it really was. There was no going back now. At last there was a set of rational explanations for the existence of life. There was no need for a creator. Atheists beamed with joy, as they now had a solid bedrock foundation from which to progress. This monumental book sent shockwaves through the world that are still reverberating to this day, such was its positive impact on rationality, reason and atheism. Theologians didn't know what had hit them. They still don't. Creationists, who lie, cheat and bully, still attempt to discredit evolution with their dim-witted, simplistic and ridiculous ideas. See, amongst many others, the acerbic and pull-no-punches *Flock of Dodos: Behind Modern Creationism, Intelligent Design and the Easter Bunny* by Barrett Brown and Joe Alston. (It should be noted in passing that Creationists claim that America was set up as a Christian nation. It wasn't. Founding fathers like Washington and Jefferson were deists and religion and state were to be kept separate.)

Meanwhile, in the United States, atheism, although arguably a slower starter than in Europe, began to stick its head above the parapets. Abner Kneeland (1774–1844) published the *Boston Investigator*, an atheistic newspaper, and was promptly prosecuted for blasphemy. The American suffragette movement had many women atheists in its ranks, as exemplified by Elizabeth Cady Stanton (1815–1902), who formed the women's movement in 1869 with Susan B. Anthony and was the author of *The Woman's Bible*, a feminist critique of the old and new testaments, and Matilda Joslyn Gage (1826–1898), who wrote *Woman, Church and State*. They began to demand better treatment from the patriarchal theists who were adhering to the sexist views contained within their book of holy fantasy. Stanton, who demanded an end to slavery, was treading on many theistic toes and was, unsurprisingly, despised for it.

Interestingly enough, it was around this time that religions entered their paranoia-based, millenarian, 'end of the world' phase, preaching apocalyptic nonsense, perhaps as a subconscious reaction to the rise of atheism and free thought. The purely invented idea of 'rapture' caught the theistic imagination. Certainly, there had been predictions about the end of the world in the past. Many had thought it would come at the turn of the first millennium (an arbitrary date, in any case) but now more than ever fear gripped the misanthropic theists. With the second millennium fast approaching, people couldn't wait for the end time.

Darwin's dangerous idea cut a swathe through everything from natural history, religion and suffrage to the rights of man. Our position in the universe was seen as almost inconsequential – an accident that undermined the misplaced theistic certainties about man's place and position in god's divine plan. This would influence numerous philosophers such as Nietzsche and Bertrand Russell, writers such as HG Wells and Mark Twain and scientists like Einstein and many others. However, Darwinism, and by association atheism, would become the focus of blame, wrongly of course, for later atrocities perpetrated by Nazism and Communism. Theologians sought to devalue the two, as they still do, by associating them with political extremism.

The Twentieth Century to the Present Day

In the first three decades of the twentieth century, reconciliation between science and religion was mooted and very nearly occurred but conservative theologians, who just could not face having to deal with reality, sabotaged it. Scientists and open-minded theologians were willing to enter into debate but, perhaps fearing further Darwinian embarrassment, hardcore theists drew a line in the sand.

The most famous clash in the early part of the century, which still has repercussions today, was the Scopes 'Monkey' Trial of 1925. It was the first time that evolution had come up against creationism in a court of law. God, it seemed, was on trial. The agnostic lawyer, Clarence Darrow (1857–1938), defender of liberal causes and opponent of the death penalty, defended teacher John T. Scopes who had, against Tennessee state law, taught evolution in a school. Darrow argued in court against the fundamentalist preacher and three-times-rejected presidential candidate William Jennings Bryan. Sadly, Darrow lost and Scopes was fined $100, the amount being waived after a technical point. The law, indeed, was an ass.

The founder of 'Objectivism', the atheist Ayn Rand (1905–1982), real name Alice Rosenbaum, was a Russian émigré who despised communism. She became an American citizen and, for a time, was a screenwriter in Hollywood. Her most famous work, published after the repeated rejection of her first book, *The Fountainhead*, was *Atlas Shrugged*, which illustrated her philosophy of laissez-faire capitalism and self-interest.

(Objectivism is now sometimes described as a cult and it is not without its fervent critics – see chapter 8 of Michael Shermer's *Why People Believe Weird Things*.)

During the 1940s, the American Humanist Association and the International Humanist and Ethical Union were set up. The United Secularists started the *Progressive World* magazine, which continued to be published until the 1970s, and Gora (1902–1975) started the Atheist Centre in India, allowing atheists from around the globe to gather together. He also organised World Atheist Meets. Countering the nonsensical idea that atheists are not civically minded, the Atheist Centre was (and still is) heavily involved with social reform. On the radio, both Robert Harold Scott in the States and Margaret Knight in Britain delivered atheistic broadcasts and received harsh criticism for their troubles.

In France, Existentialism came to prominence with the intellectuals of the Left Bank in Paris. The most famous exponents of the idea that Man is essentially alone in a meaningless and absurd universe were Jean Paul Sartre (1905–1980) and Martin Heidegger (1889– 1976). Existentialism, which had its roots in the work of Danish philosopher Soren Kierkegaard (1813–1855), argued that people were responsible for and sole judge of their own actions as they affected others. Self-aware individuals could grasp their own existence and freedom while not allowing their decisions to be constrained by anything, not even morality and reason. It had a number of variants due in part to Kierkegaard being a Christian, albeit a radical one and Sartre a Marxist.

It was during the paranoid, Cold War 1950s that atheists came under fire again. The *American Rationalist* magazine was starting its run but freethinking was attacked by the likes of delusional bigot Senator McCarthy (1908–1957) – another theist who had to lie and cheat to get what he wanted and whose ignorance destroyed the lives of many good people. This was the last great surge in which atheism was associated with communism, when disbelief in god automatically made you anti-American. (It was nonsense, of course, but the idea was to rear its ugly head again after 11 September 2001 in an alliance of neo-cons and creationists.) During the 1950s, theists in the US moved to merge church and state, something Thomas Paine and the founding fathers would have denounced vigorously. The theists wanted to put the words 'under god' in the pledge of allegiance and to add 'In God We Trust' to the dollar bill.

But atheism was not going to lie down and wither. If anything it found new strength, revitalised by unconstitutional bigotry. This strength was seen in the campaigns of the controversial Madalyn Mary O'Hair to separate church and state and her success in removing public prayer and bible readings from schools in the 1960s. It was seen in the 1970s in the setting up by Paul Kurtz of the world-famous Prometheus Press in New York to publish books on numerous freethinking subjects – not least atheism. The most famous publication of the time was (and still is) George E. Smith's *Atheism: The Case Against God* – an absolute must-read for anyone wishing to give up theism. Later in the decade, Anne Gaylor started the 'Freedom From Religion Foundation' and began publishing *Freethought Today*. One of its members, who joined in the 1980s, was Dan Barker a preacher who saw the light and gave up believing in nonsense. His journey to atheism is recounted in his book, *Losing Faith in Faith: From Preacher to Atheist*. The foundation then seeded other groups, which tied themselves into an affiliation called the Atheist Alliance, which publishes *Secular Nation*.

The US has become the new battleground (not too light a term) between atheism and theism, largely because of the rise of the bible-spouting, neo-con Christian Taliban and its attempts to undermine democracy and to inflict childish nonsense on the children of America and the rest of the world. Atheism, however, has never been stronger and, in the works of such authors as Richard Dawkins, Sam Harris and Christopher Hitchens, just three of a countless number writing about the subject today, atheism is moving from strength to strength and meeting any challenge put to it. The great strides in scientific understanding of how the universe ticks makes the position of a deity more and more untenable. Right-wingers may denounce it but they know, in their hearts, they are casting their seeds on stony ground. Atheism is now at its most progressive point in history and, backed up by science, rationality, reason and intelligence, it cannot fail.

Defending Atheism

*'If mankind would make true progress, it must be
on the basis of atheism.*
Gustave Flourens, *Science de l'Homme*, 1865

*Religion is regarded by the common people as true, by
wise men as false and by rulers as useful...*
Seneca

It must be re-emphasised that atheism means non-belief. It is not
an alternative belief system as some theists try to claim. Atheists
tend to be a disparate group who refuse to adhere to labels and,
although atheism has nothing to defend, the right to be an atheist
must be defended. Atheism is neither narrow-minded nor blinkered. It is not restrictive or destructive. It is progressive, not
backward looking. It is positive, not negative. In it there remains
hope for the encouragement of learning and the search for what
is true about the natural world and our place in it. The challenge
is not so much to make theism look foolish (it does that on its
own) as to defend the rationale of non-belief. Atheism can high-
light the deficiencies in religion and it should not be afraid to do
so. Whenever possible, it should step out into the light and make
its presence known.

Accusations of Fundamentalism

One criticism levelled at atheism is that of extremism or fundamentalism. In short, atheists are just as bad as their religious
counterparts. In a risible television documentary with a title that
reveals its ignorance, *The Trouble with Atheism*, seen on UK's
Channel 4, writer and broadcaster Rod Liddle attempted to
tarnish atheism by making just those accusations. He claimed
that atheists, and by default scientists, were just as guilty as
theists of holding extremist views. He even stated, erroneously,
that science has its high priests and its temples.

> *According to psychoanalysts, projection is the process of attributing one's
> own ideas, feelings, or attitudes to other people or objects — the guilt-laden
> adulterer accuses his spouse of adultery, the homophobe actually harbours
> latent homosexual tendencies. A subtle form of projection is at work when
> fundamentalists make the accusation that secular humanism and evolution
> are 'religions' or announce that skeptics are themselves a cult and that reason
> and science have cultic properties, a claim that sounds absurd given that a
> cult is by definition 180 degrees out of phase with reason.*
>
> Michael Shermer,
> *Why People Believe Weird Things.*

Science is not a belief system. It is not another form of religion.
This cannot be stated often enough. If it is, then the definition of
'religion' has become so broad it is self-defeating. Biologists do
not use faith to make evolution work. Evidence piles up on
evidence. A recent discovery, using the collagen protein, proves
that the common chicken is related to T. Rex, adding yet more
weight to Darwinian evolution. (Oddly enough, the god-fearing
Daily Mail on 13 April 2007, when reporting this, used the
phrase, 'supporting the belief expounded by Charles Darwin…'
This is to suggest that Darwinian evolution is just another idea,
'a belief', scraping around for something to back it up. It isn't,

it's fact.) Nor do geologists have 'faith' about the age of the Earth – they can prove it, over and over again. Science makes great strides in understanding. Religion does not. Science demands clarity, religion obfuscation.

Frank Tipler, a physicist, is notorious for mixing religion with his 'science'. Tipler who was raised a Southern Baptist is infamous for muddying the waters. In his latest book *The Physics of Christianity* he goes full throttle on the nonsense pedal. It is only when religion-obsessed scientists (a tiny minority) try to explain the myths of the bible, e.g. Christ's resurrection in scientific terms that they become unstuck. See Michael Shermer's *Why People Believe Weird Things* and eSkeptic *Blinded By Science?* Wednesday, August 1st, 2007 ISSN 1556–5696.

Liddle's approach, attempting to prove some point known only to himself, was nothing short of silly distortion. This was simply theist spin (from a non-theist apparently), aimed at soiling the opposition, intent on bringing science down to a religious level where arguments about phantom intangibles can split a church asunder. Scientific progress is built on fundamental processes (Darwinian evolution for instance) and this is where Liddle gets confused. Liddle oddly enough then gives Dawkins' *The God Delusion* a big thumbs up (see review taglines attached to the paperback version). If he has read this book then he would understand the conflict between atheism and the fundamentalist stance. Dawkins addresses the issue of so called 'fundamentalist atheism' very expertly in *The God Delusion*. If Liddle has read this book then surely he'd know.

Peter Hitchens, self-confessed right-wing monster (another man who should look up the meaning of liberal with a small 'L' in the dictionary), has made similar accusations about science, and by inference atheism, in the *Mail on Sunday*, in what seems like a one-man crusade to get everyone to listen to him. He wants a god in his image. But his views do not stand up to scrutiny. Like theists of all creeds, he makes it clear that he is very unsure as to what exactly atheism is. He himself admits to having never completed a book on atheism yet is enthusiastic in his criticism of it. Hitchens is at the silliest extreme of the spectrum. To him, it represents moral decline and social disorder. Of course, it represents neither. More recently, he's accused atheism of being behind the rise of Islamic fundamentalism. In other words, disbelief will supposedly encourage Muslim extremists to drag us all off to Mosques. In mentioning his 'western god' he displays a fine example of right-wing anxiety about the world expressed through the bias of religious narrow-mindedness. How is he in a position then to criticise that which he has no understanding of? It is safe to say that the majority of atheists have at least read the major religious books of their respective cultures. Hitchens himself decries what he and others call, 'woolly thinking' (usually aimed at left wingers) but there is nothing more wrapped in woolly thinking than a belief in a god.

Has there really been, as Hitchens suggests, a decline in morality? How can empire building, misogyny, war, slavery and the plunder of resources that made Britain 'great' be considered moral? What about the crusades, witch burning, auto-da-fes, homophobic persecution and (ghastliest of euphemisms) ethnic cleansing? These have all shown theistic intolerance writ large. Barely 300 years in all of human history have been without warfare – not a good advert for a benevolent deity. Atheists, as they are now, have been a minority throughout that time. Can Hitchens, in all honesty, really blame them for the world's ills? The list of crimes in god's name is endless – all committed in the service of so-called god-fearing morality. Hitchens has even passed comment on the fact that atheists don't have organisations like Oxfam and Christian aid (actually, they do) and lauds the work these institutions perform. Such praise is fine but it ignores the fact that, if there were a god, there would be no need for such charitable bodies. He also ignores (as do all theists) the fact that, for example, the highly secular Scandinavian countries are the most generous in helping others and have some of the highest standards of living in the world. But if there is a moral decline, why isn't his god doing something about it?

In his feeble attempts to rubbish non-belief, Hitchens readily ignores the total failure of Christianity. Christianity thrives on guilt, not love and Hitchens wants us all to feel that way. As man who claims vehemently to despise woolly thinking, he regularly falls victim to it. In one of his *Mail on Sunday* columns he asked where were his fins if evolution was right? He has failed to grasp the fact that, because of the evolution of fins into limbs, he walks around on a pair and uses the other set to wash up with or to type out his strident rantings.

If one is to state that the sky is blue (a fact), then this, by Liddle's and Hitchens' standards, could be interpreted as adopting a 'fundamentalist' scientific viewpoint. In the same way, statements such as the Earth orbits the sun at a distance of 93 million miles, Darwinian evolution is true, humans are born and then they die, the speed of light is 180,000 miles per second but may vary in strong gravity or water and the Milky Way galaxy is one of billions, could also be construed as 'fundamentalist'. Yet these are all provable and demonstrable facts and all of them are accepted as correct, even by the majority of those individuals with a strong religious conviction. Liddle, Hitchens et al stretch the meaning of fundamentalism in an effort to demean what is, in essence, a commonsense viewpoint, one not tainted by supernatural elements. To be fair to Liddle, he has little time for religious fundamentalism either but he fails to make a rational distinction between that and so-called scientific fundamentalism.

John Gray, philosopher of the LSE, in his book *Heresies*, is correct about society not being totally secular but he denounces secular humanism or liberal humanism by labelling it as nothing more than a cod religion that's nicked its ideas from Christianity (if he knew anything about Christianity, he would know it stole all its ideas as well). By lowering secularism and humanism to the status of a 'faith', he distorts the meaning of religion as well as humanism. It's that broadening of meaning we've come across before. By Gray's reckoning, everything humanity does can be reduced to the status of religion. He even dismisses atheists as evangelical and then makes the error of claiming that the Nazis were atheists. He even states, oddly, that atheism is a Victorian fossil or that, in Freudian terms, it is a form of repression. (Freud himself, incidentally, was an atheist.) How so? How on earth can atheism be repression? It's the very opposite!

Amongst other nonsensical arguments, Gray suggests that liberal humanists have repressed their 'religious experience'. In his view, atheists behave like Victorians, covering up and repressing their religious sensibilities. Well, actually, atheists don't and it is really rather stupid to say so. In fact, it is Christian ethics (with all their misogyny and homophobia) that actually repress the individual. (See *A Companion to Ethics*, edited by Peter Singer.) Not only that, they keep people at a level of immaturity, preventing them from learning. Christianity operates on a level of reward or punishment, treating the individual like a child. 'Do a good thing and god will bless you. Do a bad thing and you're going to hell!' (Even though god seems to be universally excellent at spreading misery.) Is that how we should all live?

Gray thinks that, by repressing faith (which atheists don't; they simply abandon it as empty and meaningless), human mentality will rebel into 'grotesque and illicit forms'. He says that science cannot offer a 'substitute for religious hopes'. But 'religious hopes', by which he means faith, is a meaningless term. Religious hope is nothing more than self-deception and a roundabout admission by theists that it's all hot air. As Einstein said, science is the most precious thing we have. Science shows us how reality is, not how we wish it to be. Human delusion is a dangerous thing. When was the last time prayer cured cancer? (How is it that theists get cancer? Why did the god in whom they believe so readily allow it to happen?)

Dawkins counters such arguments very well in his book, *Unweaving the Rainbow*:

> *But such very proper purging of saccharine*
> *false purpose; such laudable tough mindedness*
> *in the debunking of cosmic sentimentality*
> *must not be confused with loss of personal hope.*

Gray seems to prefer the fluffy, religious, wide-eyed idealism of a kind of Disneyland view of the human animal and its place in the universe. Religion, he argues, is hot-wired into the brain, which means, to Gray, that it must be good. We are empty without it. He longs for atheism to wither on the vine.

Gray writes:

> *We may not be far from a time when atheism*
> *will be seen as a relic of repression...*

Only in his dreams. 'Religion' may be an artefact of conscious-ness but is it a Darwinian dead end, an evolutionary cul-de-sac, or a misinterpretation of some other process? Or is it a conse-quence of self-replicating memes, which seems more likely? Maybe its basis is Freudian – springing from the child/parent bond, or a collection of neuroses. It is a universal feeling, as he states, but maybe it's negative, part of a destructive impulse masquerading as 'good' and we just don't see it in those terms. It is more likely to be a meme-plex than anything else – negative software infecting the brain. Atheism can be seen as anti-viral software when applied with reason and free thought. Despite his position and his anti-atheist stance, Gray can no more provide evidence or answers for the woefully obvious absence of god than other theists. His arguments, not atheism, wither on the vine.

The problem with religious fundamentalism is that it is not working from any perceivable facts about the real world. It is faith-based dogma, backed up by narrow mindedness, violence and hot air. It allows all kinds of atrocities to be perpetrated in its name, from flying airliners into buildings to the kind of sectarianism that splits apart whole communities. Religion makes statements about the world that are inherently false with its adherents ready to act viciously upon them.

Perhaps we should in future use the terms 'right fundamentalism' and 'wrong fundamentalism'. Right fundamentalism defines what is provable by the scientific method and is therefore comprised of factual statements about the real world; wrong fundamentalism, by definition, is the direct opposite.

Atheists, and indeed many scientists, as a result of their training, demand evidence for a deity, as well as for the other ludicrous claims of divine power such as miracles or knowledge through revelation. So far this evidence has proved non-existent. Therefore they take a position that, until otherwise proven, there is nothing to back up belief in a supreme being. The jury is out and, in all likelihood, is destined never to return.

Dawkins puts its succinctly in *The God Delusion*:

The truth of a holy book is an axiom, not the end product of a process of reasoning. The book is true, and if the evidence seems to contradict it, it is the evidence that must be thrown out, not the book. By contrast, what I, a scientist, believe (for example, evolution) I believe not because of reading a holy book but because I have studied the evidence.

This is the crux of the matter. Evidence. For evolution there is plenty. Maybe a better term than right fundamentalism would be 'evidential fundamentalism' but this only stirs up trouble. The correct stance would be to avoid using the term fundamentalism with atheism altogether since it leads to confusion and, more importantly, misrepresentation. What is more likely is that critics, who label atheists as fundamentalists, are just misinterpreting the position of the disbeliever. At the very least, theists are incorrect in their assumptions about why atheists take the stance they do.

Naysayers also fail to understand, or at least ignore, a very basic concept of science. If a cherished hypothesis turns out to be incorrect, scientists abandon it. When evidence turns up to disprove a theory, that theory is changed, dismissed or consigned to history. No fundamentalist religion has ever done that. Carl Sagan once asked the Dalai Lama what Buddhism would do if science proved a basic tenet of that religio-philosophy to be wrong. The Dalai Lama's response was heartening. His answer was that Buddhism would have to change. No religious fundamentalist, of whatever persuasion, would ever say that.

Others who label atheism as a corrupting force are Ravi Zacharias, author of a silly book entitled *The Real Face of Atheism* in which all the usual dull and tired anti-atheist statements are trotted out, including the old chestnut that atheistic morality cannot work. More general ignorance can be found in the writings of Anne Coulter (more on her later), the rabidly right-wing author of *Godless: The Church of Liberalism*, and in Jonah Goldberg's *Liberal Fascism* (talking about 'liberal fascism' is rather like talking about 'pacifist terrorism' or 'dry water'). There is also *The Menace In Europe* by Claire Berlinski, which spews out more right-wing, theistic venom. According to Berlinski, Europe is threatening the world again with its secular ways. The continent is losing its faith. In fact, the opposite is happening, particularly in the former Soviet countries where Catholicism is most definitely on the increase and there is a rise in neo-Nazi groups, which are most definitely Christian. Maybe writers like Berlinski and Coulter know when the golden age of theistic upright morality they so admire was supposed to have existed and maybe they would like to tell us.

These writers and the rest of the religious right are happy to lay the blame elsewhere rather than face up to the often negative influence America plays on the world stage. Why does much of the Arab world despise America? Why do many people in Europe have grave doubts about the most powerful nation on earth? Maybe it has something to do with the lies told to invade Iraq and the chaos that is the aftermath of the plunder of that country's oil reserves. Or America's bias towards Israel. According to right-wing theists, however, it's all Europe's fault. They are swift to denounce Islam as despotic but they want to replace it with their own tyrannical, earth-raping version of Christianity.

There is a tendency in the States at present to add the word 'fascist' to everything – fascist Islam or rather Islamo-fascists, fascist liberals, fascist atheists, fascist socialists… the list goes on. The only thing the theistic right don't think is fascist is fascism itself. It's that same policy of changing the meaning of words we've seen earlier. You sully your opponents by associating them with some other, justifiably maligned system of beliefs. Atheism is either 'fundamental' or 'fascist'. It is, of course, neither but that will not stop Coulter and her deluded chums from calling it so. Of late, American atheists have acquired the epithet 'fundamentalist' simply because they're going on marches or making protests. But they do this to keep in check the bullying tactics of right-wing theists. American atheists are behaving like true patriots by demanding that the constitution is respected and that the separation of church and state is maintained – something the opposition wants to destroy.

When it comes to crime, that other bugbear of the right, the fact of the matter is that the cities in America that have the highest crime rate are all in Republican, '*Christian*' states. (See Sam Harris's book, *Letter to a Christian Nation.*) Anne Coulter thinks atheists are 'liberals' and that liberalism is ruining the United States by being soft on lawbreakers. In reality, the only thing liberals are not doing is decrying religion enough. Liberals are too soft on theism, which allows the likes of Coulter and her band of despots, who believe the old biblical nonsense that god gave man the earth so that he could hold dominion over it, to run riot. This is why she once said, 'Earth is yours. Take it. Rape it.'

Alister McGrath is that rare thing, an atheist turned theist (it's usually the other way round). In his book, *The Rise and Fall of Disbelief in the Modern World*, although he gives a reasonable history of atheism, he then resorts to making the stupid mistake of stating that atheism is a 'religion', a deep error of judgement. Atheism, by its very nature, is the absence of religion. How can non-belief be a religion? Many of McGrath's suggestions that atheism is disappearing are down to personal opinion and nothing more. He thinks atheism is beyond its sell-by date. It isn't.

Atheism as Conspiracy?

The great mass of the people… will more easily fall victim to a big lie than to a small one…
Adolf Hitler, *Mein Kampf*

It has served us well this myth of Christ…
Pope Leo X

There is a growing trend to weave fanciful stories, which play shamelessly with Christian beliefs and ancient legends. There is no respect for history and they deny the truth, the authenticity of the Christian faith.

Father Raniero Cantalamessa
Pope Benedict XVI's personal priest
(Quoted in the *Daily Mail* 16 April 2006)

As we shall see, the quote by Father Cantalamessa is a thoroughly nonsensical statement. It was made during the throes of sweating and puffing in the church that followed the phenomenal success of *The Da Vinci Code*, a book that was said, by theists, to be part of something sinister aimed at undermining the church... cue dramatic music... an atheist conspiracy!

The 'atheist conspiracy' is a thoroughly odd idea. Both Rowan Williams, the present Archbishop of Canterbury, and John Sentamu, the Archbishop of York, both support this nonsensical silliness. If it was just a story, why did they get in such a tizz? Much of this, of course was fallout from Dan Brown's novel. The book was, to no one's surprise, criticised by the Christian power base worldwide for blasphemy when all it did was take an already established version of the Christ myth (see *The Holy Blood and The Holy Grail* by Baigent, Lincoln and Leigh) and weave a populist story around the possibility that Jesus Christ was a family man (the ultimate advert for family values, surely?). This was claimed to be part of an 'atheist conspiracy' to bring down the church but plainly it was nothing of the sort. Whatever one's criticisms of *The Da Vinci Code,* at least it allowed its readership to question things that had been presented as 'facts'.

Some facts!

There is of course no evidence that Jesus Christ was a historical figure. There is no unanimity about the time and place of his birth. It cannot be proven that he was born on 25 December – the idea that he was stems from a rewriting of old pagan beliefs. No one is sure what year he was born. Matthew suggests it takes place in Herod's time but Luke offers us the period under Quirinus, ruler of Judea – 14 years after Matthew's date. In an odd defence of this, theists have argued that this conflict was a deliberate ploy so that the infallibility of the scriptures cannot be denied. Tertullian, an early Christian writer said in his *De Carne Christi (On Christ's Flesh)*, 'it is certain because it is impossible...' Yes, that's right. Contradictions mean it's all true. Couple that with the fact that a great many of the early Christian writings were either lies or downright forgeries and we are left to wonder whether *The Da Vinci Code* is that bad after all.

Peter: We all love the bible in this house.

Francis: Really? What's your favourite book of the bible?

Peter: Umm ... the one where Jesus swallows the puzzle piece, and the man in a big yellow hat has to take him to the hospital.

Family Guy

Early Christian apologists even had the audacity, amongst other literary crimes, to rewrite the works of the pagan Porphyry, chief exponent of Neoplatonism and a critic of their religion, to make it sound as if he was giving them the thumbs up when he was doing nothing of the sort. They cobbled together a pro-Christian manuscript called the *Philosophy of Oracles* and slapped Porphyry's name on the bottom. They even demanded the destruction of other critical works. The eighteenth century church historian Mosheim writes, 'The Christian fathers deemed it a pious act to employ deception and fraud...' Milman, another, later historian, writing about early Christian missionaries, states, 'Pious fraud was admitted and avowed.' Bishop Ellicott in the late nineteenth century admitted, 'It was an age of literary frauds...' A good deal of classical literature by writers such as Plato and Aristotle also suffered at the hands of 'pseudepigraphers' (people who falsely attributed works) and it is now known that most of the books of the New Testament have suffered from the clandestine, inky hands of forgers.

Joseph McCabe (1867–1955), a one-time Catholic priest, subsequently saw the error of his ways and became an atheist. He realised it was all a pack of lies and wrote numerous books (more than any other atheist, in fact) on the absurdities and atrocities of the Catholic Church. His books include *The Forgery of the Old Testament*, *Religious Lies*, *Did Jesus Ever Live?* and *Do We Need Religion?* Even someone steeped in theistic tradition could see it was all nonsense.

The Alexandrian Jew and scholar, Philo, visited Jerusalem during the time that Jesus was supposedly working his miracles. Oddly enough, Philo, in all his works, makes no mention of anyone called Jesus. He's never heard of him. At one point, he highlights the distinction and meaning between the two names Hosea and Jesus, defining the name Jesus as 'saviour of the people'. Here would have been a great moment to mention Jesus the supposed worker of miracles. '*Oh, by the way, there's this bloke here who doesn't get his sandals wet.*' But Philo never does. Even Origen, head of the Christian school of Alexandria and successor to Clement, when he was defending Christianity from Celsus, the great rationalist and medical writer, had to resort to appealing to pagan mythology to prove that the story of Christ was real. He could offer not a scrap of evidence but he said that it was no more incredible than the stories of the Roman and

Greek gods. (So, not true at all, then.) Origen wrote himself into a trap by saying, about history, 'It is often very difficult and sometimes quite impossible to establish its truth by evidence which shall be considered efficient.' In other words, he didn't have a clue whether Jesus existed or not. Not one of the early founding fathers of the Christian church could prove the existence of their prime mover so they resorted to cheating.

Justin Martyr, another early Christian apologist (100–165 AD), said much the same thing in item 21 of his First Apology, a philosophical defence of his beliefs, which he addressed to Emperor Antoninus Pius. He wrote, 'When we say also that the Word, which is the first birth of God, was produced without sexual union, and that he, Jesus Christ, our teacher, was crucified, died and rose again, and descended into heaven, we propound nothing different from what you believe regarding those whom you esteem sons of Jupiter.'

Even Paul, the greatest apostle and author of early Christianity, knows nothing about a miraculously born saviour. He makes no mention of a virgin birth (an idea that may have been the result of an error in copying manuscripts, anyway) in any of his 13 epistles. And these are older than the Gospels. The idea was unknown to Paul, as it was to all Christians at that time. The virgin mother and the Holy Ghost (whatever that is?) were not part of the 'tenets' of the new cult. Paul is ignorant of the miracles as well as the message of Jesus. Could he really preach the 'new way' without knowing anything of the Sermon on the Mount or the story of rich men and the eye of the needle or the use of bread in large outdoor picnics? Not once in any of his writings does Paul mention anything connected to what theists believe the biblical messiah did. In fact much of Paul's epistles have a distinct flavour of the Persian cult of Mithraism to them.

When Paul was teaching, the Gospels had yet to be written.

When the early church, was first established, the Gospels had yet to be written. Repeat, yet to be written... This is desperately important and worthy of an Oliver Stone film. The church was without its founding text. The Jesus of the Gospels was not yet in existence. No image of him appeared until about the eighth century and then it was a nondescript and beardless face in the style of Byzantine art. His image and PR owed more to Alexander the Great – the archetypal god king – who influenced Judaism, Christianity, Buddhism, Hinduism and Islam. The stories surrounding Jesus were cobbled together from a whole host of sources including paganism, Zoroastrianism and Mithraism (the birth of Mithras, it should be noted, was accompanied by attending shepherds and Mithraic rites included baptism and communal meals). The figure of Jesus also drew on such mythical characters as Adonis, Osiris and Dionysos. Take Tammuz, the ancient god of the Sumerians and Phoenicians, for example. He had been born of a virgin, died with a wound in his side and rose again after three days from his tomb and left it open with the rock rolled aside.

It is clear that Jesus was an invention. He was a new figure-head for a brand new cult set up and led by Paul, the ancient equivalent of Joseph Smith, L. Ron Hubbard or Peter Griffin, who founded the 'Church of the Fonz' in *Family Guy*. People fell for it then as they fall today for the childish ideas of miracles, conspiracy theories, Bible codes (according to Michael Drosnin, author of *The Bible Code*, the world was supposed to have ended in 2006 in a nuclear holocaust – did we miss something?) and ancient astronauts.

This is just the tiny tip of an enormous theistic iceberg constructed out of fibs. Why did the early church use such tactics? Why lie, cheat and employ forgery? Was it simply because Jesus did not exist and the early Christians resorted to a conspiracy out of desperation?

The present day suggestions that attacks on religion form an atheist conspiracy is nothing new, of course, but it is another fine example of how resistant established religions are to change and to criticism. More importantly, it reveals how fearful theism is of close and reasoned questioning. Theists know that their belief system is nothing but a house of cards waiting to collapse.

In early 2007 Pope Benedict XVI announced that, just like that, he was abolishing limbo, a mythic realm where font dodgers were said to go. Infants have to be baptised with magic water so that they can be cleansed of some idiotic notion of original sin, which was all the fault of a non-existent character called Adam. If the Catholic Church is now happy to accept evolution (Pope John Paul II's address to the Pontifical Academy of Sciences in 1996 suggested that even the church was hedging its bets), then it must necessarily deny Adam as part of a creationist myth. So what's all this nonsense about original sin? More importantly, if the Pope can just remove limbo, something that had been part of theistic teaching for nearly a millennium, just how easy is it to get rid of the rest of it? Limbo was nothing more than a threat, designed to compel compliance with church teachings. No further proof is needed that theism is nothing more than a dogmatic fantasy invented to scare people.

Grandpa Griffin: You're a good woman, Lois. Perhaps you won't burn in hell after all. Maybe you'll just go to purgatory with all the unbaptized babies.

Peter: There you go, Lois, you love kids…

Family Guy

Atheist conspiracy? It is plain for all to see that the conspiracy lies with religion, which attempts to keep the faithful cowed under the dictatorship of myth. Atheism revels in its free thought, beyond the restrictions and the demeaning quick fix imposed by religion. To suggest a god created everything condemns humanity to a life of meaningless drudgery and ritual – in other words, slavery. It is not atheism that limits the mind but theism. If we accept god as creator, then what's the point of doing anything? If we accept an absurd concept, we stagnate. No questions are asked about how the universe works because it's all down to god anyway. How feebly narrow-minded is that? Our perceptions are distorted by the rose-tinted glasses of divine majesty. The cosmos doesn't look like the ceiling of the Sistine Chapel and it is only through science and free thought that we will see it as it really is.

The conspiracy lies not with, or in, atheism but within theism itself and how hollow and empty the words of Father Raniero Cantalamessa, the Archbishop of Canterbury and numerous others sound.

See *Did Jesus Exist?*, and *The Jesus Legend* by GA Wells; *Jesus the Magician* by Morton Smith; *The Encyclopedia of Biblical Errancy* by C. Dennis McKinsey; *Out of the Desert?: Archaeology and the Exodus / Conquest Narratives* by William H. Stiebing; *The Book of Q and Christian Origins* and *Who Wrote the New Testament? The Making of the Christian Myth* by Burton Mack; *Gospel Fictions* by Randel Helms; *Laughing Jesus* and *The Jesus Mysteries* by Timothy Freke and *The Truth About Jesus, Is He a Myth?* by MM Mangasarian.

Guilt by Association

'I shall remain a Catholic for ever...'
Adolf Hitler

Theists like to use 'guilt by association' when condemning athe-ists. For example, the evangelist and homophobe Stephen Green of the Evangelical Alliance (whose website declares it wants to defend freedom of speech but can't stand anyone saying anything anti-Christian and bangs on endlessly about 'blasphemy' – itself an expression of free speech) uses this technique when lunging inexpertly at atheists. His feeble approach, which he has used on TV programmes such as the BBC's *Heaven and Earth Show*, is to trot out the hoary old cliché about Hitler being an atheist. Therefore all atheists, according to Green, must be Nazis. Atheism is the root cause of Nazism (or is it vice-versa – who knows with these people?).

Was Hitler an atheist? In fact, atheism, throughout history, has been a minority view in German society. In Southern Germany and in Austria (Hitler's birthplace), the social introduction, *'Grüss Gott'*, translates as 'God's Greetings'. Not something atheists would use. They were also burning Sigmund Freud's books in Berlin in 1933. Freud thought religion to be an illusion born from neurosis. He didn't believe in god. Why would atheists burn atheistic books? In fact, the Nazis burnt them because of Christian-fuelled anti-Semitism. *'What progress we are making.'* Sigmund Freud wrote, 'In the middle ages they would have burned me. Now they are content with burning my books.'

By Green's reasoning listening to Wagner would automatically make you anti-Semitic, watching *The Sopranos* would make you a mobster and, presumably, enjoying *Thunderbirds* would make you a wooden puppet.

Hitler was actually raised a Catholic and attended schools of that faith. So were many others in the Nazi leadership, including Himmler who was born into a pious Catholic family. Alfred Rosenberg, the Nazi ideologue, was a pagan and probably cavorted with druids in nudity-based ceremonies. Hitler, as well as being Oedipal, suffered a messiah complex and identified with Christ very strongly (see the BBC Timewatch documentary

Inside the Mind of Hitler – describing the work done by Walter Langer in his book *The Mind of Adolf Hitler*). The Führer was also deeply fascinated by the occult as well as by all kinds of daft myths and ideologies about the *übermensch*. He dreamed about idealised Christianised knights, riding to the aid of some romanticised Germany. So too did Himmler whose SS hierarchy occupied and rebuilt Wewelsburg Castle to become the focus and HQ of a cod-religious, knightly order.

Hitler would talk for hours about Catherine Emmerich, a visionary who described the Passion of Christ in lurid detail, as if she was there, and he was also heavily influenced by Adolf Josef Lanz, aka *PONT* (Prior of the Order of the New Temple), who published *Ostara*, a magazine for people who preferred their history with a distinctly Aryan flavour, and believed the master race was about to be reborn. Lanz often wished that god would simply wipe various people from the face of the earth. This included all the usual suspects from the big bumper book of individuals theists like to hate.

Many Christians became Nazis and, since Catholics and Protestants made up the majority in German society, therefore the German army must necessarily have been made up of members of those two major faiths. *Gott Mit Uns* (God with Us) was etched into Nazi belt buckles. There were padres or *Feld Bischofe* and chaplains or *Heeresgeistliche* on the field of battle to administer to the souls of the master race. Army chaplains had a gold cross hanging from a chain around their necks. There were two versions – one for Protestants and one for Catholics. Indeed, the 'cross' was heavily used throughout German military orders.

More damningly still, Hitler thought he was doing god's work. On a visit to Bayreuth, Hitler met the Wagner family at their villa. Also staying there was the mad-as-a-March-hare

Englishman, Houston Stewart Chamberlain, Wagner's son-in-law. Chamberlain had written a book entitled *Foundations of the Nineteenth Century*, which claimed that the fate of civilisation lay in the hands of (guess who?) ... the Teutonic race. Chamberlain, who thought himself as a John the Baptist figure, announced to all and sundry that Hitler was god-given, praised him as the messiah and asked the almighty to protect the saviour of Germany. Hitler lapped it up.

Hitler did start out by sticking the boot into Christian ideology, especially his own faith Catholicism because he thought it was too soft on the race issue. (Even Bismarck, in his *Kulturkampf* of the 1870s, had attacked Catholicism with the so-called *'Falk laws'*, which had forced Jesuits to flee the country and led to the incarceration of numerous bishops.) But then Adolf changed his tune. Article 24 of the Nazi party programme stated that there should be, 'liberty for all religious denominations in the State so far as they are not a danger to...the moral feelings of the German race. The party stands for positive Christianity.' During a speech Hitler made at the Reichstag in 1933, he stated that Christian faiths were, 'essential elements for safeguarding the soul of the German people'. Countless Protestant pastors welcomed the Nazi regime with open arms. This was, in all likelihood, the result of anti-Semitism – the Jews were stigmatised as Christ-killers, an idea which many Christian theists still think true even today.

It was not long before the Nazis fell into bed with the Vatican, although they promptly fell out again. The Pope at least sensed impending trouble in Germany and made the slightly odd statement that he saw, 'the threatening storm clouds of destructive religious wars' gathering over Germany. In later years, there would be accusations that the Vatican, under 'Hitler's Pope', Pius XII, knew of the Holocaust but kept quiet about it or, more damaging still, denied it had ever happened. The British Home Office, in a memo at the time, called Pius XII a moral coward.

Many theists in Germany, particularly Protestants, were heavily influenced by the persistently miserable Martin Luther (who suffered horribly from constipation which might explain a lot – see *The Devil's Doctor: Paracelsus and the World of Renaissance Magic and Science* by Philip Ball, Arrow 2007), a man who said that Christians should destroy all reason within them so that they could swallow the word of god (or any other nonsense offered). The founder of Protestantism was a rabid bigot and anti-Semite whose words were full of a kind of malice unequalled until the Nazis came along. Luther, too, had wanted Germany free of Jews and wanted them deprived of 'all their cash and jewels and silver and gold'. He also demanded that, 'their synagogues or schools be set on fire, that their houses be broken up and destroyed...' It sounds all too familiar.

Nazis also despised homosexuals and freemasons. Doesn't this have an all-too-familiar theist ring to it? Both groups, together with atheists and Jews, are seen as lurking behind every supposed anti-royalist, anti-theist, leftie-based conspiracy that conspiracy theorists have dreamed up. (In passing, it should be mentioned that in numerous illustrated bibles, usually published in America, Jesus is portrayed in very Aryan terms – long blond hair, blue eyes, pale skin and unashamedly Nordic. It's very clear what the publishers of these books want their messiah to be. Non-Jewish. The best examples of this can be seen on those ghastly 'collectible' plates on the back of tabloid colour supplements or the deliriously cheesy pamphlets handed over by Mormons in which Jesus as hippy farmer, clutching a domestic ruminant, is portrayed in decidedly WASP terms. They only just fall short of wrapping him in Old Glory to present that all-round, right-wing American messiah look.)

The Nazis set up the German Christians Faith Movement whose leader was Ludwig Müller, army chaplain of the East Prussian Military District. They embraced Nazism and wanted all Protestants gathered together into one institution known as the Reich Church. Of course, this didn't run smoothly and, when it came time to elect a bishop, all hell broke out until Hitler, in a radio address, urged the election of '*German Christians*'. Müller was duly elected bishop.

In 1933, more nonsense kicked off during a rally held by said German Christians. One Dr. Reinhardt Krause wanted the Old Testament dumped because, as he said, it was full of 'tales of cattle merchants and pimps'. He also wanted the New Testament re-written so that it corresponded with National Socialism. In short, he wanted, '*One People, One Reich, One Faith.*'...One true religion...

The minister of Church affairs was a lawyer by the name of Hans Kerrl. In a speech he made, laying it on thick to Protestants and Catholics who didn't get the Nazi message of Race, Blood and Soil, Kerrl said:

> *The party stands on the basis of Positive Christianity and Positive Christianity is National Socialism. National Socialism is the doing of God's will. God's will reveals itself in German blood...True Christianity is represented by the party, and the German people are now called by the party and especially the Fuhrer to a real Christianity. The Fuhrer is herald of a new Revelation.*

During the Second World War it became clear to Hitler that Nazism and Christianity were falling out of favour with each other. The Nazis wanted Christianity swept aside in favour of the old gods and the introduction of a new paganism. Churches were to be emptied of all Christian regalia and, in their place, artefacts of the Hitler Cult were to be raised. *Mein Kampf* was to be the holy book – the word of god. This new religion was to be known as the National Reich Church. Article 19 of its agenda stated:

> *On the altars there must be nothing but Mein Kampf, to the*
> *German nation and therefore to God, the most sacred book…*

And what of the Nazi collaborators in Catholic France and Vichy who deported nearly 80,000 Jews to the camps? Or other 'Christian' countries in Europe who welcomed the Nazis as an excuse to solve their own 'Jewish problem'? In Vichy France, certain elements of the Catholic Church backed the regime as they did in Italy during the years when Il Duce strutted his stuff. Even the Pope gave Mussolini his blessings and said that the dictator rose to power as a result of divine providence.

Of course, there were many Christians who opposed Nazism and did their bit to stand up to the regime by helping to rescue Jews. (Some Jews were spared if they married Christians as if, somehow, this made them better people.) While Protestants lined up to vote for Hitler in greater numbers than Catholics, there were still dissenting factions who were warning of what was ahead. But this is not the issue here. The issue is whether or not Hitler's regime was an atheistic one. It wasn't.

To make the tired old claim that Hitler and his cronies were atheists and that Germany was an atheist regime is totally wrong. It may have been anti-Semitic and eventually (although this is debatable) anti-Christian but it was certainly not anti-religion. It was about as far from atheism as it is possible to be. (See Nicholas Goodrick-Clarke's book, *The Occult Roots of Nazism*.)

Another line of attack involves linking Hitler with Nietzsche (1844–1900). As the philosopher was an atheist and Hitler sought inspiration in his work, it is assumed that Hitler was an atheist. Wrong. Nietzsche's philosophy was that man should give up the gods to enable him to evolve; to become *übermensch*. Hitler took this profoundly odd idea of 'superman' out of context. When Nietzsche wrote, 'I teach you the superman. Man is something to be surpassed', he wasn't talking about tall, blue-eyed, blond-haired, muscle-bound gentlemen from Dusseldorf.

> *God is dead; but looking at the way Man is, there*
> *will probably be caves for thousands of years in*
> *which his shadow will be seen.*
>> Nietzsche, *The Gay Science.*

In the battle of Monte Cassino, one of the most famous battles of the Italian campaign in the Second World War, two names should be mentioned. Fridolin von Senger und Etterlin, commanding general of XIV Panzer Corps and a lay member of the Benedictine Order (i.e. a Catholic) and Lt. Colonel Schlegel, commanding the engineer detachment of the Hermann Goring Panzer Division, helped to save the various monastery treasures and the library from destruction. Schlegel assisted Dom Gregorio Diamere and the monks by supplying numerous trucks to transport the items they rescued to Rome.

Schlegel wrote:

> *The Abbot now proved himself the gracious, upright*
> *man that he was. He begged me to help the monastery*
> *and said that he would do all he could to support my*
> *rescue work.*

Is this the work of a 'destructive atheist'? Even if Schlegel was an atheist, it proves the contrary to what theists like to promote about the Nazis. If Schlegel was a god-fearing man, it just proves that there were Christians in the German military who wanted to protect religious iconography and literature. (See *Cassino,*

Anatomy of a Battle by Janusz Piekalkiewicz.)

Special attention should be paid to the most famous symbol of the Nazis – the swastika or *'fylfot'*. This was an adaptation of the old pagan symbol for the sun. And we must not forget, of course, the use of crosses in medals and decorations. Why would atheists have a use for symbols such as this? Atheists have no need for icons and images.

If Hitler felt in any way atheistic – and this is highly unlikely since the man quoted Christian texts in his speeches and was deeply motivated by the occult – it does not follow that all Nazis were atheists or vice versa. To claim so is a failure in reasoning. It is clear to most historians that Germany, in the Nazi era, was run by a messianic cult that absorbed its tenets, as all cults and religions do, from a variety of sources and these included Christianity. Nazi ideology was a mixture of paganism, occultism, mythology, pseudo-science and religion. It was not atheistic.

Before we leave the Nazis, let's just consider one last example – the activities of one British Conservative MP, Archibald Maule Ramsey, a violent anti-Semite and leader of the neo-Nazi Nordic League. In 1938, freethinkers and atheists from around the world met in London. Despite the fact that there had been a similar meeting four years earlier without so much as a raised voice from anyone, the 1938 gathering faced public outrage. The meeting was seen as a two-finger salute to empire, monarchy and patriotism. Of course, it was nothing of the sort but the Nordic League decided that free thought and atheism were part of a communist plot to undermine society. MI5 even started sniffing around the congress, paying particular attention to the completely innocent South Place Ethical Society and the National Secular Society.

Ramsey brought a bill before parliament, the Aliens

Restriction (Blasphemy) Bill, in June 1938. Get this. The meeting of atheists was seen as potentially damaging to the already strained relations with Nazi Germany. Into the fray came the Catholic Church and other theists who sided with Ramsey. The bill passed its first reading as a large number of MPs backed it. Thankfully the government saw sense and kicked it out. (See *BBC History Magazine* Vol 5, no 9, September 2004.) Let's just remind ourselves what happened here. A *Nazi* in the UK thought atheists were bad news because they didn't believe in god. It should be noted that many, if not all, modern neo-Nazi movements are Christian.

If atheists are not Nazis, then they most certainly are communists. According to the evangelical right, that is. But surely atheists can't be both fascist and communist at the same time? This just goes to prove how stupid it is to view atheism in political terms – especially in terms of political extremism of both left and right totalitarianism. Yes, there are atheistic communists. There are also atheistic capitalists, theistic communists and god-fearing industrialists. It would be interesting to see what right-wing theists make of capitalist atheists.

So what of communism?

Communists espoused atheism – Karl Marx famously said, in his *Critique of Hegel's Philosophy of the Right,* that, 'Religion is the opiate of the people' – and therefore many of those with heavy religious leanings claim that atheists are necessarily communists. They assume that being a communist is, in itself, inherently 'evil'. In the US during the 1950s, suffering under the cross-dressing hypocrite J. Edgar Hoover and the foaming-at-the-mouth paranoid Senator McCarthy, communism was demonised by people on the Right. They then went on to stigmatise socialism, liberalism and atheism. Language was misused to stultify thinking and to tar these ideas with the same brush as communism. Many on the Right were (and still are) Republican Christians so it was (and still is) in their interest to denounce anything that wasn't right-wing and theistic as thoroughly as they could. It serves the men in power to decry anything that might upset their bank balances, their mindsets and their memberships of their golf clubs.

Billy Graham, the evangelical loudmouth who found god on the eighteenth tee of a golf course, is a figure on the right who has befriended every Republican president since the 1960s. Graham was convinced that communism was the work of the devil. Any popularity Communism might have had was, of course, linked to the virulent repression it suffered from state and church and from people much akin to Billy Graham who revelled in a fire-and-brimstone supernatural tyranny. Graham and other pinko-hating preachers thought anyone not a Christian or anyone who criticised the faith was by default a communist.

Stephen Glover, writing (badly) in the *Daily Mail* of 26 April 2007, uses this trick to have a pop at Richard Dawkins. Glover, eulogising Boris Yeltsin, the teetering old sot and erstwhile bad conductor who also gave us Putin, praises the man for seeing off the 'communist atheists' of the past and restoring Christianity to Russia for the first time since the Czars. (The truth is that he didn't really.) The article implies that Dawkins and other advocates of atheism are either commies or at least sympathetic to the big 'evil C'. If Russia is all moist-eyed over Christianity now, why are so many eager to see the return of the old order? The country, now capitalist, is not exactly liberated anyway and seems to be lurching towards totalitarianism again. Or, at the very least, in some areas there are stirrings of far right politics with a distinctly theistic smell to them.

But here we are in 2007 and Glover is still using the wearily inane and 'tiresome guff', to quote AC Grayling, to denounce atheism. It's clear that Glover is another one who really doesn't understand what atheism is. If he did, he would stop tying it into communism. He is, however, writing for a right-wing newspaper that still harbours dozy dreams of god and empire. It sometimes seems as if this is all theists have in their prehistoric '*armoury*' – denunciations that use bad examples to infer guilt through irrelevant associations with fascism or communism. As George H. Smith wrote in *Atheism: The Case Against God*:

> The irrational and grossly unfair practice of linking
> atheism with communism is losing popularity and is
> rarely encountered any longer except among political
> conservatives.

Let's be clear from the start, Stalin (real name Joseph Vissarionovich Dzhugashvili) did what he did because of his extreme politics not because of his atheism. He was a sociopath, a sadist, bully, a gangster and a terrorist who loved political repression and enjoyed revenge and murder. He ordered his purges because he had corrupted the ideologies of communism not because he employed the rationalism of free thought. If he was an atheist, he certainly did not behave like one. Stalin himself was a paranoid and anti-intellectual lunatic. He once answered a question about his most enjoyable pastime and replied:

> My greatest pleasure is to choose one's victim, slake
> an implacable vengeance, and then go to bed.

With the greatest will in the world, this could never be described as the outcome or the direct result of atheism. More importantly, it is not how an atheist thinks.

In Freudian terms our personalities are constructed in youth.

Like Hitler, Stalin was regularly beaten by an alcoholic father. He was raised in a religious family and actually trained to be an Orthodox priest but was kicked out of the seminary in Tiflis (now Tblisi) for mouthing off about Marxism. Later, this religious background would manifest itself in his virulent anti-Semitism, which led to the execution of 19 Jews in 1952 for being part of a 'Zionist Conspiracy'. These were words straight from the heart of Christian extremism and Stalin's actions were odd for a man who was, through his dictatorship, ruling a society based on a brutalised version of the ideas of Marx, a Jew. Stalin also despised the 'Jewish' Mensheviks. (It is interesting to note that, although Marx was himself an atheist, his communist ideology, which worked on the assumption of the inevitability of progress, was rather godlike in its optimism. Something always missed by theists.) It should also be noted that anti-Semitism is not born of atheism.

In the same way as Hitler, Stalin made use of a 'cult of personality' – in his case, that of Uncle Joe. Not only was he *Khozyain*, the Boss, he was also presented as an avuncular and down-to-earth character. Every despot seems to want to be seen in this way. Take that other so-called atheist state, North Korea. North Korea is nothing more than an organised, military-backed cult, worshipping Hollywood fan and star of *Team America:World Police* (2005), Kim Jong Il – the Dear Leader. It is no more atheist than the Catholic Church. The Dear Leader helped to develop the cult that built up around his father, Kim il Sung (1912–1994), and proclaimed him the 'Eternal President', an expression that has a distinctly religious feel to it. North Korea is also a mixture of traditional beliefs, Buddhist and Chondoism, a monotheistic religion of Chondogyo – Society of the Heavenly Path – (also known as Tonghak) – a combination of Christianity, Buddhism and Confucianism.

Christianity coming from the introduction of Catholicism in the seventeenth and nineteenth centuries.

Stalin ruled, like Hitler, with a rod of iron ('*Stalin*' in Russian means 'man of steel'), using secret police and strongarm tactics to cow the people he governed and he was not averse to employing murder whenever he thought it was required. Again, it should be emphasised that these are not the actions of an atheist. Stalin demolished churches because of his paranoia not his atheism. The church was only one of many sources of opposition. If a dictator wants to rule successfully, he must remove all resistance and religion was seen as the last bulwark of the old regime. Of course, the church was also wealthy and Lenin, Stalin's predecessor, saw it as a war chest. Some 2,700 priests and 5,000 monks and nuns were killed by the regime and there were 1,400 confrontations between the Red Army and believers. Many were shot on trumped up charges of counter-revolutionary behaviour. Yet these numbers along with his purges, in which a vast number of intellectuals, atheists and genuine scientists (as opposed to followers of pseudo-scientists like Lysenko) were also shot, pale into insignificance against the deaths caused by religion.

Russian historian Roy Medvedev made an interesting comment about Stalin. He wrote, in *Let History Judge*: 'We cannot equate Stalinism with socialism, Marxism or Leninism – no matter how imperfect these doctrines might be in some respects. Stalinism is the sum total of the perversions Stalin introduced into the theory of and practice of scientific socialism.' Later in his regime, Stalin chose to appeal to the religious side of his people in order to unite them against Hitler.

The church was not eliminated in Soviet Russia and, in fact, it was tolerated insofar as it helped to maintain morale. Midway through the Second World War, Sunday was once more the day of rest and permission was given to restore damaged religious artefacts. The League of Militant Godless, a group of boisterous thugs formed in 1925, was almost dead in the water by 1942. During Easter that same year churches in Moscow were permitted to hold candlelit processions. In pre-communist times, the Russian Czars were in cahoots with the church to repress the people and the church taught people to accept this as part of god's work. (Why are atheists constantly cited as the root cause of revolutions? In reality, popular uprisings are the work of angry populations, grown sick and tired of living off nothing but stale bread while the elite swans around in luxury, deciding that they have had enough and wanting to make some swift changes. No repression, no revolution.) This was also true, in the past, of the clergy of the Church of England who were constantly in league with the monarchy to suppress the people.

To claim that atheism was the sole cause of Stalin's actions is to ignore a whole host of other more credible reasons for them. Stalin was an insane monster and a good place to start to look for motivation for his actions is his personal psychopathology. It should also be noted that any political ideology is a belief system in itself and, at the risk of repetition, it should be emphasised that atheism is non-belief. Capitalism and communism have a set of rules that govern their processes so, whether a country adheres to fascism or to Marxism, it does so out of the belief that the particular political ideology it favours is workable. Instead of removing religion from society altogether, the communists actually employed the same techniques. There were a great number of religious elements to communism – as there are in any overarching political system. Communists had their 'holy' places and their 'churches' – the body of Lenin was, like the body of Pope John Paul II in Catholicism (or indeed as Chairman Mao still is), the subject of countless pilgrimages and statues and iconography were as much a part of the communist regime as they are of the church's rule. The various symbols of Soviet Russia and communism – the sickle, the hammer and the stars – were, of course, images of a political cult that bore resemblances to religious ones. Remember, atheists have no need for ceremonies, rituals or grand 'politico-religious' theatre.

China too seeks to root out religious faiths, such as Falun Gong, for instance, but it does so because they are a threat to the power base not as a direct result of non-belief. China is not exactly a true communist state anyway. Maoism was, of course, yet another political cult. Mao, like Hitler and Stalin, employed the cult of personality to distort politics into a pseudo-religion. Any dictatorship needs one to survive. Hitler, Stalin, Mussolini, Pol Pot, Sadam Hussain et al, all relied on that process. Interestingly enough China's official religions are in fact Confucianism, Taoism, Buddhism, Christianity and Sunni Muslim. It is not an atheistic country – in fact there has never been a solely atheistic nation.

The country is now the fastest-growing economy in the world and will come to dominate the twenty-first century. It behaves much like other capitalist countries particularly in the way it treats overseas workforces such as the miners of Africa. Its human rights record and its lust for land-grabbing from the peasant farmers is the result of pure greed, not atheism. China wants to compete in the world markets and it will remove any hurdles that appear in its path. This is not to say that it is right to repress religious freedom but the repression should not be seen as an atheistic one. It is political. It should be mentioned in passing that, for thousands of years in pre-'communist' China, the people had never heard of Christ and yet they managed to create one of the greatest societies ever seen in the history of the world. Confucius (551–479 BC), who said much the same as

Jesus, predated the man by some 500 years. And Hsun Tzu (300 –230 BC) said morality comes from society not the supernatural.

What of Marxist Pol Pot (real name Saloth Sar, 1925–1998) and the Khmer Rouge? Surely Pol Pot and his fellow Cambodians were atheists? The young Pol Pot was sent to a Buddhist wat, a kind of religious school, and then to a Roman Catholic School. His Marxism, with its emphasis on no possessions, no desires, destruction of the individual and so on, was heavily influenced by Theravada Buddhist thought. Much of the motivation behind Pol Pot's brutal regime was indeed Marxist but the Buddhist influence is usually forgotten. The Buddhist clergy happily worked for the Khmer Rouge and Pol Pot was supported by the (Christian) West as a bulwark against Soviet-supported Vietnam. But no one blames Buddhism for his regime. It's always, of course, Marxism.

Pol Pot also played on his people's desire for a return of Khmer greatness again after Vietnam and Thailand nearly did for Cambodia. This longing harked back to the thirteenth century when the Angkorian Empire stretched over most of the region. Over the ensuing centuries it was swallowed up by neighbouring countries. Pol Pot offered Cambodians a new, strong 'Khmer' identity. Like Hitler and Stalin, he played on national insecurities to ease his transition into power.

Maybe Hitler and Stalin's Catholic upbringings played a greater part in their actions than theists are willing to admit. They were both anti-Semitic; both had cults of personalities constructed around them; and what they uttered was held as gospel. They wanted to be seen as saviours, messiahs, and godheads of their respective nations. Ultimately, all the Nazis did was to replace one religion with another – the Cult of Aryanism. The idea of a master race, racial crusades, the commitment to the sacred soil of the Fatherland, Aryan faith, Aryan ritual and belief in Hitler as messiah – these are not the beliefs of atheists. In fact, why did Hitler not embrace Marxism? Marx was an atheist. Hitler was rabidly anti-communist, a contradiction surely if he really were an atheist and believed communism to be an offshoot of non-belief.

Thankfully, the ridiculous misrepresentation of atheism as linked to communism and Nazism has lost a great deal of ground of late but it still surfaces from time to time in the god-promoting literature of the Christian right. Atheism, it must be emphasised, should not be seen as an automatic offshoot of communism, as the theist so often concludes. George H. Smith, in his excellent book, *Atheism: The Case Against God*, writes:

> *An atheist may be a capitalist or a communist, an ethical objectivist or subjectivist, a producer or a parasite, an honest man or a thief, psychologically healthy or neurotic. The only thing incompatible with atheism is theism.*

Richard Dawkins puts it more succinctly in his barnstorming *The God Delusion*:

> *Individual atheists may do evil things but they don't do evil things in the name of atheism...*

Exactly!

An atheist may deny the Holocaust ever happened – it does not make Holocaust denial a tenet of atheism, nor does it mean that all atheists are Holocaust deniers. But this is just the kind of sleight of (under) hand misdirection theists like to use.

Any 'evangelista' using the argument that 'Hitler or Stalin were atheists and therefore atheists are evil' has not thought it through, and is either ignoring the facts or simply being dim. Both Hitler and Stalin were despotic and lunatic dictators, full of mad ideas, who often worked hand in hand with religion to provide justification for their lust for power. Their actions were due to psychotic paranoid behaviour not atheism. People under both dictators lived in abject fear, especially dissidents and free thinkers. Repression such as this is not evidence of atheism. It is political tyranny. In many respects, the dreams of uniting humanity in a 'paradise' on Earth that both dictators shared (although they differed wildly about the political paths that would lead to those dreams being realised) were nothing more than a reworking of the beliefs of monotheistic religions.

Certain theists, usually pro-royalist right-wingers, often travel further back in time to the days of the French Revolution to find supposed examples of the evils of atheism. They like to point out that the Jacobins were nothing more than a bunch of atheistic thugs who brought misery to the French people. The Jacobin Club, which first came together in a former Dominican convent, was formed to protect the gains made in the early years of the revolution. They were united in their belief in the equality of all citizens. They policed the markets, were a focus for public virtue and raised supplies for the army that defended the revolutionary state. In elections of 1791, they increased their power in the revolutionary assemblies and they became a rallying point for those keen to continue the revolution. They led the government from mid-1793 until mid-1794. In many ways, the Jacobins were idealists. Robespierre, a radical Jacobin, may have been the figurehead of 'the Terror', but he also wanted to free the slaves in the French colonies and championed universal suffrage.

The causes of the French Revolution, in which the Jacobins were so heavily involved, were many, but the fundamental reason it occurred was that the peasants were sick of their oppression and tired of the arrogance of Louis XVI's court and of the fact that indolent brandy-soaked aristocrats lived high on the hog while they starved. To state that the French Revolution was down to pure atheism, or that the actions of the Jacobins were the result of disbelief, is a gross misrepresentation of the roots and causes of the revolution. The church at the time was in cahoots with the ruling classes and did nothing to further the cause of the underprivileged. The people saw it as a tool of repression and that's why it suffered. Of course, they also saw it as the source of superstitious nonsense. In Rod Liddle's *The Trouble With Atheism*, he seems to suggest that countries were better off with a repressive elite focused on the twin ideologies of monarchy and Christian religion. If that is the case, why did the populations rise up in Russia and France? Precisely because of that repressive double act, working in tandem to hold the people down.

The French Revolution owed much of its intellectual inspiration to the Enlightenment and the thinkers of that era draw the fire of theist critics. When Diderot and his colleagues in the mid-eighteenth century wrote their secular *Encyclopaedia*, with its anti-superstitious and anti-religious stance, it could have been designed to stick in the craw of theists and this is the genuine source of their antagonism to the period.

The Enlightenment has its fevered critics but, in most respects, they miss the point and stupidly blame it for all kinds of heresies. However, as Ernst Cassirer, Peter Gay and AC Grayling make clear, the Enlightenment was, 'a complex movement of thought', and it established a 'set of aspirations for the improvement of mankind's lot'. Peter Gay has gone further by writing that, whenever there is an intellectual quest for the good throughout history, it has instantly come up against superstitious theism. Before Nazism and communism, before even the days of the French Revolution, the atheist would have been tainted by any number of accusations – immorality, satanism, sedition, anti-monarchism and so on.

Numerous 'Hitlers' and 'Stalins' have always blighted history but, as AC Grayling highlights, never before had technology been available as it was in the twentieth century for them to fulfil their manic dreams on such a large scale. However, atheism was never the prime motivator for their genocidal politics. On the contrary it was always some form of cod-messiahship and the misplaced delusion of manifest destiny.

All this, of course, begs one question of theists who promote these misrepresentations of atheism. We cannot condone the deaths that occurred but we can ask where god was in all this. Why, when people were being slaughtered en masse, was there no divine intervention? Why didn't god stop it? Especially, if it was supposed atheists that were up to no good. What an opportunity to show the unbelievers up. But, no. Never. Not one instance of divine intervention to halt a dictatorial genocide.

There is also something deeply troubling about a society that seeks or demands a messiah because existing within this misplaced desire and weakness are the seeds of a willingness to be ensnared by a dictatorship.

See Simon Sebag Montefore's *Young Stalin,* Michael Burleigh's *Sacred Cause* and *God Created Lenin* by Paul Gabel.

The Religious Wrong

Chris: What do you do at a Young Republicans meeting?

Alyssa: We help those who already have the means to help themselves. Also, we perpetuate the idea that Jesus chose America to destroy non-believers and brown people.

Family Guy

We should invade their countries, kill their leaders and convert them to Christianity.

Anne Coulter on Afghanistan.
Website of the National Review.

Anne Coulter, the frothing right-wing polemicist and author, in a speech at the Conservative Political Action Group, wanted all liberals to be killed. This doesn't seem to fit with her belief in the commandment, 'Thou shalt not kill.' Is Anne Coulter Christian at all? She doesn't sound as if she is. In fact, none of these right-wing bigots do. What is it with these theist fundamentalists who spout 'god is love' and then say they're going to kill homosexuals, liberals and atheists while insisting women are second-class citizens? Or who say, 'god has given you free will', but want you dead if you exercise it?

This is the woman, remember, who said 'rape the earth' on Fox Network's talk show *Hannity and Colmes*. Does she really believe this? Do she and the others who mouth off like her represent the real and true face of Christianity? Why are these people always right-wingers when the religion to which they cling is, if we're going to mix political and religious terms, predominantly a 'left wing' ideology? Why are they so upset? If they believe that god made everyone, then he made liberals and homosexuals and atheists. He made everyone they hate. Do they, by inference, hate their god?

This, then, is the supposedly warm and loving, 'god loves everybody', 'family values' tolerant culture of the theistic community in the States. It's the hypocrisy of people who want others to follow the Ten Commandments but who are themselves happy to ignore them at every possible opportunity. This is the right wing '*Christian*' culture of the States. But is it wrong to condemn all Christians on the basis of the behaviour of Anne Coulter and her ilk? Well, the truth of the matter is... yes. Anne

Coulter is behaving like a true theist. 'All national institutions of churches, whether Jewish, Christian, or Turkish', wrote Thomas Paine in The Age of Reason, 'appear to me no other than human inventions set up to terrify and enslave mankind, and monopolize power and profit.'

Yes, each faith has its less belligerent members but each religion, be it Christianity, Islam, Judaism, Hinduism or whatever, claims to be tolerant when, in reality, dogma requires that its adherents assume themselves to be superior to others. In churches, mosques, temples and shrines throughout the world the mantra is, *'we're right and they're wrong'*. Of course, they all despise atheists but at least the spite of the extremists is not hidden behind timid phrases of faux acceptance. Islamic fundamentalists want to introduce sharia law to the countries in which they have made their homes, countries that have no desire to accept it, because they think it's the will of Allah. His will trumps that of any other god. Even Islamists of different factions (Sunni and Shia) consider the other to be following the lower path. Hindus and Muslims regularly clash. Protestants and Catholics spent decades blowing each other up in Northern Ireland. All these confrontations were and are down to the dogmatic belief 'that we are better than them'.

Michael Moore, in his book, *Dude Where's My Country*, suggests that American conservatives, particularly frenetically religious ones, are actually on the back foot because of fear. Humorously, he suggests that they shout, foam at the mouth and make stupid racist statements, usually on talk radio or the Fox News channel, simply because they know they are in the minority. Here's hoping. They are living in fear that their god might actually be a liberal. How these people love their bigotry. But then Jesus (if, indeed, he existed) wasn't averse to a bit of racism either. He rejected anyone who wasn't Jewish. He only came to save a few people not everyone. As a Jew himself, Jesus said he was there to save his people and his people only. As he says in the New Testament, 'Go nowhere among the Gentiles and enter no town of the Samaritans, but go rather to the lost sheep of the house of Israel'. (Matthew 10. 5–6).

Perhaps the religious right are actually being true to their faith, then.

Do they distort their theism into bigotry or is it simply that theism is bigoted by its very nature? The simple fact is that theism is bigoted – full stop. In their treatment of women, homosexuals, other faiths, atheists, freethinkers and critics, theists reveal that they all hate those who don't see it their way. If you argue with them, they tell you that you are deluded and try to convert you. As an experiment, when next theists call at your door with their fairyland stories, tell them you follow any other religion but their own and watch their faces. Tell them you're an atheist and watch their eyes glazing over or their hands reach for their crucifixes. If you tell them you're Jewish, watch their malice grow. And then consider when was the last time an atheist came to your door to lecture you on your wrongdoing.

In Louis Theroux's BBC documentary film, *The Most Hated Family in America*, broadcast, interestingly enough, on 1 April 2007, the Phelps family aka The Westboro Baptist Church, led by an obviously bitter, twisted and hate-filled patriarch, took their incomprehensible, homophobic message to the streets. The overriding feature on display in the film was the irrational, twisted logic to which religious extremism is subject. As far as the 70 or so members of the Phelps's tiny church were concerned, they were saved and the rest of the world was doomed to burn in hell for all eternity. They even startled the hosts of the right-wing Fox network, which as viewers of the documentary film *Out Foxed* will know, takes some doing. What arrogance! What hubris!

Yet how typical of the religious who make exclusive claim to the 'truth', a word that has been spectacularly misused by those who preach such hatred from the pulpit. The Phelps, like others, pull off the doublethink of believing that their god created everything but then despising most of what he created. Then they claim to be doing their god's work to put it all right. (See also the excellent *Keith Allen Will Burn in Hell*. UK's Channel 4, broadcast 21 June 07)

This is where religion always falls down. Apart from the legerdemain of its twisted logic, so much of religious doctrine can be interpreted in any way that fits the narrow-mindedness of its followers and this, in turn, leads to hatred and violence. That the world suffers from such mental primitivism is an insult to our species.

Religion and paranoia about the outside world seem to be two mindsets that have gone hand in hand throughout the history of the US. Perhaps that is why all the major conspiracy theories come out of that country – often on the back of theistic fear. The supposed machinations of secret societies intent on creating a one-world order are always liberal, demonic, Jewish, Masonic and/or atheistic and, although the country was set up by deists who were keen to keep religion the private activity of the citizen and not a tool of state, America has been populated by fundamentalists.

Despite the vehemence of the religious right and despite what anyone may tell you, atheism is liberation from bigotry.

Religion in Mind

Religion is an illusion and it derives its strength from the fact that it falls in with our instinctual desires...

New Introductory Lectures on Psychoanalysis.

God is nothing more than an exalted father.

Totem and Taboo.
Sigmund Freud

Religion is a by-product of mind and therefore it can be studied within the realms of neuroscience. Voices in the head, spectral lights and all the other elements that go to make up the religious experience are all felt through the senses which are, in essence, the outward manifestations of the brain as it experiences and attempts to make sense of the outside world.

Freud thought religion was all the result of the mind and wrote, in *Obsessive Actions and Religious Practices* (1907): 'In view of these similarities and analogies one might venture to regard obsessional neurosis as a pathological counterpoint of the forma-tion of a religion, and to describe that neurosis as an individual religiosity and religion as a universal obsessional neurosis.' He also states that belief in a god is a response to human helpless-ness: '...the terrifying impression of helplessness in childhood aroused the need for protection – for protection through love – which was provided by the father; and the recognition that this helplessness lasts throughout life made it necessary to cling to the existence of the father, but this time a more powerful one.'

This is borne out by the incessant use of terms like, 'our father', 'god the father', 'god and his children.' etc. This is a display of little more than mental immaturity.

In a letter to Freud, Romain Rolland, the French author and musicologist who won the Nobel Prize for literature in 1915, coined the term 'oceanic feeling'; to describe the mystical, cosmic emotion that is the true source of religious experience. Unable to find this feeling in himself, Freud's view, in *Civilisation and Its Discontents* (1930), was that religious emotions are regres-sion, 'to an early phase of ego-feeling' when the infant at the breast was unable to distinguish its ego from the external world. In Freudian terms, the breast is also a representation of a person's wishes, impulses, fantasies and anxieties.

In psychoanalysis there is the term 'ritual', which was borrowed from religion. Here the patient fends off obsessional neurosis with a ritualised series of repeatable actions used as a counter-magic to fantastic fears. In other words – religion.

To say that religion is incapable of scientific study is a persistent fallacy or, at the very least, a potentially harmful and limiting stance. Many who commit to a faith say that religion is beyond the instruments of science; that knowing the mind of god is beyond the bailiwick of scientists. This is a false statement and one that merely reveals the fear and overly defensive posturing within the religious community towards scientific 'meddling' in a subject in which it believes it has no business. But science does have the right. To limit the scientific method because of religion and succumb to NOMA, the idea of Non-Overlapping Magisteria propounded by Stephen Jay Gould, is simply insulting to human experience and to the human quest for knowledge. If confident of god's existence, surely religious believers would welcome scientific truths to back up their claims. Rigorous methodology endorsed by learned papers in *Nature* would surely clinch the argument in favour of a deity.

If one can measure the rudiments and the workings of the universe and, as the religious say, god either is the universe or created it, it follows that he is part of the equation and should be understandable in terms of celestial mechanics, physics and chemistry. Yet no particle accelerator, no spectrogram or Hubble telescope, in fact no scientific instrument at all, has ever detected the presence of the almighty. Surely, if humanity's aim is to 'discover' god, as some claim, then by his works shall we know him. He is conspicuous by his absence.

Of course the usual, often vitriolic, retorts to such arguments are that god is spirit and that puts him beyond the realm of such study. God, it seems, is in constant retreat into the shadows. One should expect more, surely. If god is knowable, as countless billboards outside churches claim, then he is just that, by whatever method we use to seek his presence.

Atheism as Narrow-mindedness and the Poetic Tradition

Poetry is the mother of superstition
Thomas Sprat,
History of the Royal Society

One of the many criticisms of atheism is that it is, by its nature, narrow-minded. The unbeliever and the sceptic have closed their minds to possibilities. This is, of course, completely untrue. Atheism is the rejection of the idea of gods and the supernatural after open-minded consideration of the facts. The search for truth cannot be undertaken by closed minds. The atheist has rejected such things because they do not stand up to scrutiny and vigorous testing. Reason alone has brought the atheist to his or her position. To understand a subject we must give it critical scrutiny and then decide whether it is a conceptual dead end or something worth pursuing. Religion is such a conceptual dead end because it fails to back up its claims with anything tangible. Science accepts the inevitability of change whereas religion does nothing of the sort. The tenets of faith are seen as inviolate, unmoving and locked in dogma. Its theological feet are firmly planted in the past.

Atheists have not reached their position because they have closed minds. Religion has been rejected for greater understanding. At best, it was a detour, one which proved to be a dead end, on the long road to the comprehension of how the universe operates. Atheists find faith deeply wanting and move on.

In reality, it is religion that has an entrenched position that denies the myriad range of possibilities. The moment anything new that appears could threaten it, the novelty is met by a fierce rebuttal. It has taken until very nearly the present day for the Catholic Church to accept that Galileo was right and that evolution is fact. The latter was disputed until 1996.

It is the misperception of atheism as narrow-minded that leads its critics to accuse it of destroying spirituality or a sense of wonder and awe in the face of nature. Countless theologians of all faiths have denounced atheism as ridding humanity of its sense of mystery. They think it is preferable to have a narrow, 'question nothing' view of creation rather than to go and find out what's going on. Poetry is a description of that mystery and probing too deeply rids humanity of its sense of the numinous. This is a false perception. Atheism does not deny the poetic tradition. A sunset can still be moving or a symphony emotional without belief in a god.

When Roger Bacon (1214–94) says, 'I had rather believe all the fables in the Legend, and the Talmud, and the Alcoran, than that this universal frame is without a mind,' he falls into the trap of self-delusion as comfort. He would rather see a world comprised of homespun nonsense than lift the veil and see the truth beyond. He cannot tolerate, or is frightened of, an amoral universe or the materialistic view that man is not born of a divine plan. If it does not fit into his world-view, then it must be wrong. This is an act of genuine hubris, arrogance and indeed cowardice that finds its counterpart in the thinking of modern day creationists. Bacon, like his modern, but defiantly retrogressive fellow believers, has put human beings at the cosmological centre of things and cannot entertain the fact that humanity is far from being the focus of a divine plan. He takes comfort in a dazzling array of lies.

Another woeful myth is the idea that somehow science and therefore atheism destroy or cripple the imagination. If science casts light into the shadows and reveals the 'monsters' there to be nothing of the sort, then somehow we, as a species, have lost something special. There is a whiff of arrogance about this, too. The idea that we should all remain in the darkness in order, somehow, to experience life at a deeper level is nothing short of intellectual tyranny. Humanity, according to Bacon and his ilk, should remain locked into a perpetually darkened room to experience shadows that play about the walls and marvel and wonder at the mysteries. To question them is to steal their magic and leave the observer empty. Nothing could be further from the truth. Theism condemns us to walk in a perpetual twilight world.

Dawkins elaborates on this idea in his *Unweaving the Rainbow* in which he puts to rest the fallacy once and for all. Keats was alarmed by the way science was destroying the beauty of a rainbow by explaining how it worked in real and materialistic terms. Newton had, according to him, unwoven it into nothing more than prismatic colours. The poet was wrong. Understanding how that glorious arc of colour was formed led directly to spectroscopy, which, in turn, has taught us so much about the universe. It has revealed greater things for the human mind to consider, not lessened our ability to wonder. Each scientific discovery opens our minds further while religion demands that we close them off. Science has embellished the poetic tradition not destroyed it.

Dawkins puts it simply:

> And the heart of any poet worthy of the title Romantic
> could not fail to leap up if he beheld the universe of
> Einstein, Hubble and Hawking.

Carl Sagan, in *The Demon-Haunted World*, illustrates just how
much more thrilling and beautiful the universe is beyond that
darkened room. In conversation with a taxi driver, Sagan demolished all the false notions, his shadows, that the man seemed to
have about the world – all the pseudo-science and the beliefs
about Atlantis, Nostradamus and UFOs.

Sagan writes:

> And yet there's so much in real science that's equally exciting, more myste-
> rious, a greater intellectual challenge – as well as being a lot closer to the
> truth.

Sagan then goes on to give us a series of starling scientific facts
that are beyond the limited imaginations of those who profit
from nonsense such as the taxi-driver believed and they prove to
be far more interesting and stimulating. They show us that the
cosmos is far more complex and thrilling than the limited imaginations of soothsayers and priests would have us believe.

There is no conflict between poetry and atheism or, indeed,
science. Shelley understood this. Despite his atheism, immor-
talised in his pamphlet of 1811 *The Necessity of Atheism,* which
caused his expulsion from Oxford, he was and still is one of our
greatest poets:

> Earth groans beneath religion's iron age
> And priests dare babble of a God of peace.
> Even whilst their hands are red with guiltless blood.
> Shelley, *Queen Mab*

Poetry from an atheist there.

Shelley was influenced by the radical writings of William Godwin, author of such books as *An Enquiry Concerning Political Justice* (1793). Godwin was a civil liberties campaigner who stated that morality was defined by reference to the greatest good. He argued that selfish actions bring less pleasure than beneficial ones, an idea now recognised in the natural world as highlighted by Dawkins in *The Selfish Gene* and Matt Ridley in *The Origins of Virtue*, books which refer, in the broadest terms, to the tendency for species to act altruistically for the benefit of the gene pool. Survival requires acts of benevolence. In other words, the natural world does not require a moral code handed down from on high to act kindly. It is built in at the genetic level.

William Blake, the man who as a child saw Ezekiel sitting under a tree and wanted Jews to convert to Christianity, also felt threatened by the onslaught of science and yearned for Newton's sleep so that the fantasies of his imagination would remain unharmed. He also thought that to question the natural world was a surefire way to damnation. As he wrote in his *Auguries of Innocence*:

> *He who shall teach the Child to Doubt*
> *The rotting Grave shall ne'er get out*
> *He who respects the Infant's Faith*
> *Triumphs over Hell and Death...*

How narrow-minded! How petulant! How limiting! For Blake, Newton was nothing short of 'satanic' for opening our minds. Blake wanted the mysterious and the unfathomable to remain that way. He was influenced at first by the crazy mystic Emanuel Swedenborg and his 'Church of the New Jerusalem', but Blake's writings were to become more reminiscent of the work of the eccentric German theologian Jakob Boehme who stated that God was neither good nor evil but had two states, that of wrath and that of love. Evil was a necessary hurdle that humanity had to conquer to fill up the empty spaces left by fallen angels in heaven. Blake thought that heaven and hell, instead of standing against each other, should merge as part of some creative force. That's all well and good but it's quite simply wrong. Atheism does not take away anything except misplaced idealism and it certainly does not rid us of our poetic tendencies.

See Richard Dawkins' *Unweaving the Rainbow* for further thoughts on the poetic tradition.

Science and the Quest for God

A close examination of the validity of the proofs adduced to support any proposition is the only secure way of attaining truth, on the advantages of which it is unnecessary to descant: our knowledge of the existence of a Deity is a subject of such importance that it cannot be too minutely investigated; in consequence of this conviction we proceed briefly and impartially to examine the proofs which have been adduced.

Shelley, *The Necessity of Atheism*

Putting aside Stephen J. Gould's idea of NOMA (Non-Overlapping Magisteria), why should a god not be open to measurement and scientific study? Our understanding of the world increases exponentially year after year. The macro- and the micro-worlds expand. Surely, at some point, we are bound to bump into god. Should we have already done so? The obvious answer is, yes. But we haven't.

Theists are swift to attack science on two fronts. Either they claim that it is trying to demean god or they say that it will never find him anyway, so why bother? How can science demean god? If a god created the universe he would relish the fact we are discovering the processes he employed (and supposedly ignores when working miracles).

Surely, theists would welcome this. They should, by rights, welcome the discovery of god with open arms. Religions should be backing science one hundred percent. If they are confident god exists, then why not have science prove it once and for all? Yet they resist such attempts at knowledge, claiming it to be blasphemous or a result of arrogance on the part of the scientific community. Undoubtedly, at the heart of this (and, if they were honest, they would admit this) there is fear, fear that their god becomes more and more impossible to justify.

Should science discover a god theists will be the first to trumpet its discoveries. What if science unearths not one god but many deities lurking 'beyond the veil'? How will the theists feel then? Of course, this isn't going to happen. If a god existed, evidence for his existence would have been found by now. If, as creationists maintain against the odds, the Earth is a product of his work there should be evidence of the maker. How is it that, in all our study, not a single scrap of evidence to back up a biblical creation as ever surfaced?

How can some theists believe devoutly the nonsense that the bible is pure fact, the word of god, when it states that the Earth was made over six days and, according to the calculations of some theologians, 4,000 years ago? (Incidentally, why did an omnipotent god need to rest on the seventh day? Isn't that a sign of weakness?) All scientific evidence points to a world formed from a stellar disk nearly five billion years ago.

How can they deny evolution when the evidence is all around them? There is nothing more destructive to silly thinking than evolution. It has blasted apart simplistic mindsets and ridiculous belief systems. It has brought humanity, in many respects, to a fork in the road and shown it the way to progress. We can quite happily allow creationists their own wrong path to darkness.

'Science has opened up large dimensions of reason,' Pope

Benedict XVI has written in his book Creation and Evolution, 'and this has brought us new insights. But in the joy at the extent of its discoveries, it tends to take away from us dimensions of reason that we still need.' What are these dimensions of reason we still need? Reason is reason. The Pope's statement makes no sense. It is, at best, a sop to modern scientific thinking and it smacks a little of fence-sitting. The Pope accepts science but can't quite let go of the idea that religion can say something about the universe. It can't. Science takes nothing away other than a myopic religiosity, which should be thrown away as a meaningless tool.

A god, if he is part of the universe, can be found through the scientific method. Just what do theists have to fear by objecting to the search? If god is part of, or creator of, the universe, then he can be found using the scientific method. Yet fearful theists like to push him further into unobservable realms, 'beyond' science, claiming that he is unknowable and should be left that way. Are they running scared? Yes…

See Victor Stenger's *God: The Failed Hypothesis*

Objections to Blasphemy

The blasphemy laws are the legal protection of nonsense. Why is there not an equivalent of the blasphemy laws for science? The reason is that science can take any criticism levelled against it. That's how science, and therefore our understanding of the universe, continue to develop. Factions of scientists do not engage in sectarian violence to the death because one group believes in the Steady State theory while another believes in the Big Bang. Scientists do not picket films that have a perceived anti-scientific stance. There were no howling mobs outside cinemas showing *I Robot*, *The Sixth Day*, the very silly *Signs* or the hokey old twaddle of the truly appalling *The Exorcist*. There is a great deal of anti-science in the world but scientists do not congregate waving placards and threatening death to anyone who denies the existence of Einstein. Nor do they place *fatwas* on those who deny quantum mechanics. They have better things to do.

But religion, when it comes up against criticism, nine times out of ten, resorts to some form of violence to defend itself. This has been a common occurrence throughout history. If play-wrights, filmmakers, authors and artists cannot make genuine criticisms of religion, then we are all in deep trouble. If we want to criticise all faiths, then we must be at liberty to do so and those same faiths must be willing to accept that criticism in whatever form. One film or opera on TV will not bring down Christianity. One book will not destroy Islam. Reason does not attack the man but it does question his beliefs. However, theists (and some on the Left) merge the two. They are convinced that, by launching a broadside at a faith, the rationalist is attacking the race of an individual. For example, by questioning the Koran, atheists are somehow making racist comments about Muslims. They most certainly are not.

Is it not high time that blasphemy laws worldwide were torn up? Science does not need them and nor should religion. Unless, of course, it feels that its position is totally untenable and needs all the help it can get. Religion by its very nature, deals with fanciful notions, creation myths, and faith, and it is preached by an array of often half-baked figures who make great claims that subsequently prove to be worthless. Religion has taught us nothing about the universe. Its one undeniable gift has been to show us how gullible humanity is. Religion has brought us pain and suffering on a grand scale. Science may have built the atomic bomb but it was men of god who dropped it. If we are not allowed to criticise religion and its failings on a grand scale, then we all suffer. Science is always under attack but it does not hide or resort to aggression. It does not retreat behind the scientific equivalent of the blasphemy law.

What Is Wrong with Religion?

Objections to 'Faith'

Now hope that is seen is not hope, for who hopes for what he sees?

Romans 8:24—25

There are thousands of variations of religion, which suggests that its roots lies in something inherent in the human animal brain, albeit a misinterpretation of some natural by-product of natural selection but the fact that there are so many variations attests to its falsehood. They can't all be right. It is perhaps an artefact of expanding consciousness or an expression of humanity wondering about its place in the universe but one that is observed through religious falsehood. We all may share a sense of the numinous but it doesn't mean we're all right about its interpretation. Why should Christianity be any more relevant than Navaho beliefs? Only because certain men say it is and nothing more.

When backed into a corner the theist will then produce what he considers to be his trump card. That trump card is 'faith'. By using the word 'faith', the theist is actually agreeing with the atheist. *'You're right, there is no evidence that proves my god exists.'* Faith is the last redoubt, the last rampart to hide behind. As there is no evidence for god, the atheist is told, often in patronising tones, to accept the vacuous idea of faith, which is nothing more than wishful thinking. Faith is a desire, a hope that something might turn out to be true against all evidence to the contrary. A theist may believe that god exists, may have faith, but nothing is there save dreams and phantoms.

Bertrand Russell said:

> We may define 'faith' as a firm belief in something for which there is no evidence. When there is evidence, no one speaks of 'faith'. We do not speak of faith that two and two are four or that the earth is round. We only speak of faith when we wish to substitute emotion for evidence.

Something quite bizarre as well as revealing happens when a priest lectures his congregation about faith. What he or she is saying is that it's better to believe through faith than evidence because there isn't any of the latter. It's an admission that the answers are unavailable. Faith is a magician's trick, a sleight of hand used to confuse and befuddle. Derren Brown, in his television programmes, tells the audience that all he does depends on mind tricks and psychology. If only the priesthood could be that honest. Interestingly, in one of his shows, Derren Brown used psychological techniques to make believers out of atheists and atheists out of believers. If it's that easy, surely religious experience has a more prosaic source than believers contend. Put simply, theists have been duped.

When a man who, say, is supposed to have killed his wife is brought before a court, the jury demand evidence for the charge – even a jury made up entirely of theists. No one would accept the accusation of murder if the prosecution said they had no evidence to back it up but they did have faith that he was the murderer. Nothing else, just faith. Not a court in the land would find the alleged murderer guilty. But this is exactly what happened in the witch trials. The prosecution in such cases were simply acting on faith. Look at the destruction their faith caused. If all the theist has is faith, they have nothing at all.

Dan Barker in *Losing Faith in Faith: From Preacher to Atheist* wrote:

> *The only proposed answer was faith, and I gradually grew to dislike the smell of that word. I finally realized that faith is a cop-out, a defeat — an admission that the truths of religion are unknowable through evidence and reason. It is only undemonstrable assertions that require the suspension of reason, and weak ideas that require faith. I just lost faith in faith. Biblical contradictions became more and more discrepant, apologist arguments more and more absurd and, when I finally discarded faith, things became more and more clear.*

Faith is often a motivator for war. We have seen this recently in the invasion of Iraq. President Bush talks about faith in his actions and faith in god who told him to invade. Stirring up the national psyche on the basis of faith is both idiotic and lethal. People die over unsubstantiated nonsense. (How can that be moral?) Faith can supposedly move mountains but why does that have to include mass slaughter? Through faith, humanity can be duped into religious or political compliance.

God's Benevolence?

Charity shall cover the multitude of sins…
Peter. 4: 8

Is God willing to prevent evil, but not able? Then he is not omnipotent. Is he able, but not willing? then he is malevolent. Is he both able and willing? Then whence cometh evil? Is he neither able nor willing? Then why call him God?

Epicurus

Theists claim that many of their charity organisations look after the needy, the hungry and those less fortunate. This is admirable indeed but does it not involve an implicit statement that their god is pretty useless? If he was a benevolent entity, why are there all the hungry children dying by their thousands every day? Some claim that the suffering are there to teach man a lesson – to be better people. Evil teaches humanity the ideas of good. This is a disgusting concept – that most of the world should suffer in order for others to learn from their misfortunes. This excuse is the last refuge of the worst kind of theistic apologist.

As Douglas E. Krueger writes in *What is Atheism?: A Short Introduction* (a must read):

> God must not be too bright, on this view, if he can't think of any way to impart knowledge of good other than to slaughter billions of people throughout human history. If god is omnipotent why can't he just put the idea of good into our heads, without killing someone?

How easy would that be, for a god? If he wants us to worship him as a benevolent deity, then why all the death and destruction, often done in his name? In the universe of an omnipotent, loving deity, all would be well. If, as the old expression has it, there are no atheists in foxholes, how is it that god allowed the country to be at war in the first place when thousands of people, including theists, would necessarily die?

One of the oldest and most obvious forms of evidence for the non-existence of god is the prevalence of evil in the world. How can a deity or deities who claim to be all-powerful, and benevolent, allow such horrors to continue. Theists have tied themselves in knots to explain this but have yet to come up with anything remotely like a common sense answer. They never will. The old cop out – that 'it's just god moving in a mysterious way'

– is lazily employed. The more stupid argument is that god gave us evil so that we can be better people. Innocents have to die in order to make us better individuals. It would be hard to find anything more blindly arrogant than that belief. Three-year-old children die lonely deaths, far from home, at the hands of murderers just so we can learn about god? Six million Jews, homosexuals, intellectuals, atheists, and handicapped people die in the gas chambers so we can know god? A suicide bomber sets off his bomb in a crowded market so we can understand god? This is truly despicable thinking and brooks no excuses.

It should be noted that theists like to attribute the word 'evil' to events such as tsunamis, volcanic eruptions, floods and droughts. These are not evil. They are part of the natural processes of the Earth. A devil does not stoke magma beneath Mount Etna. These occurrences are what they are – amoral events in the natural world – and labelling them as evil provides further evidence of humanity's ridiculous and juvenile predilection for anthropomorphising everything.

Religion as a False Construct of Myth

The Christian religion not only was at first attended
by miracles, but even at this day cannot be believed
by any reasonable person without one.

David Hume,
An Enquiry Concerning Human Understanding.

The very meaninglessness of life forces man to create
his own meaning.

Stanley Kubrick

We have seen how, in the very short period of time since 1947, the UFO myth has been blown out of all proportion. The reporter who spoke of Kenneth Arnold's experience of witnessing 'strange craft' near Mount Rainier in 1947 – the event which kickstarted the modern UFO craze – was the one who described them as 'flying saucers'. Arnold did not. It would be interesting to see how things would have turned out had the reporter said 'flying oblongs' in his radio broadcast. Would 'flying oblongs' have become the norm of observed phenomena? Distortions are often the root of myths and legends – and of religion.

In the case of flying saucers, a mistake, (much like the idea of the 'virgin birth', or *The Great Commission* i.e. the big monotheistic religions just out to convert people which is nothing more than a mistranslation of the Greek word, matheteuo – to teach), has developed into full-blown myth. The whole flying saucer 'mystery', like all pseudo-scientific and religious beliefs, is the result of one long game of Chinese whispers. Take the Roswell incident, for example. Not only is this now a massive money-spinner but also a whole religio-philosophy has been built up around something that never happened. A myth was born and, over the relatively short time frame of 60 years, it has become a legend far greater than the sum of it parts. The Roswell incident has been explained – it was the consequence of a top-secret nuclear detection system under the code name Project Mogul – but there are countless believers out there who refuse to accept this and are on their own quest for the 'truth'.

People have great difficulty in reaching, or perhaps are unwilling to reach, consensus about something that happened in less than the span of a lifetime. The Kennedy assassination is another classic example. How infinitely more difficult is it to say with certainty what happened two thousand years ago? The passage of time has allowed the myths that make up religion to propagate, develop and evolve until the sources are lost, the truth (if ever there was any) confounded, muted and conspired against even more thoroughly than the truth about the events of Deeley Plaza in 1963. To use any religious book as a reliable source of history is profoundly wrong.

Religion, as a creation, behaves very much like the *Star Trek* universe or Middle Earth. A basic set of characters and ideas are drawn up which are then added to over the years by fans, adherents etc. Plots are discussed and debated, character motivations highlighted and pondered, and the morality at the heart of the show or book takes on great significance. The true meanings of the programmes or stories (if any) deepen as time progresses. Star Trek fans meet up and swap icons of the show. There are even some deluded theists who, in one of Christianity's countless spin-off stories, believe that one day they too are going be 'beamed up'. *Star Trek* probably has greater relevance to the real world than religion. In many respects, it was not afraid to tackle social issues of all kinds – from acceptance of homosexuality (something the church won't always do!) to the basic rights of man. And one only has to watch documentaries such as *Trekkies* to see how seriously followers of the show take it – Klingons doing charity work!

What about the Land of Mordor? Does it exist? There are many books that refer to such a place. There are films that also back up this claim, as well as websites and computer and role-playing games. So Sauron's a real entity then? Or the ring of power? Some Tolkienites perhaps wish all this to be true; some might actually believe it to be. But is Middle-earth a real place? Well, no. Of course not, and it would be madness to claim that it is. But why stop there? Writers, filmmakers and fans for over 60 years have added to the characters and the history of the make-believe realm, beefing up its 'reality'. Who is to say that religions might not spring up from Tolkien's world?

But the bible's full of real places, the theists claim. So is *Star Trek* – San Francisco, the Solar System, the galaxy. Does Captain

Picard really exist? How about Adam or Noah? In short, why should one set of fairy tales be taken as (pun intended) gospel truth while others are seen for what they are – invention. Religion offers comfort? So does *Star Trek* to countless numbers of fans. So does any myth-based construct. What makes religious myths any more believable? Nothing.

The freethinker WS Ross (1844–1909), who became an atheist after reading the bible during his studies for the ministry, wrote:

> *Jack and the beanstalk was just as suitable for the nucleus*
> *of a religious system as Christ and his cross; but the one*
> *has been taken and the other left.*

Exactly.

Will Self's novel, *The Book of Dave*, is about a London taxi driver who, 500 years in the future, becomes the unwitting instigator of a religion based on writings to his son that he left buried in the garden. This is probably nearer the truth in reflecting the source of their own holy book than any theist would admit.

There is something dangerous and sinister about myths being used to execute great crimes against humanity. What if people used *Lord of the Rings* as an excuse to murder people of short stature? Silly example? Maybe not.

Just Why Does the Church Fear Atheism?

> *Peter pumpkin head came to town*
> *Spreading wisdom and cash around*
> *Fed the starving and housed the poor*
> *Showed the Vatican what gold's for*
> *But he made too many enemies*

Of the people who would keep us
On our knees...

XTC,
The Ballad of Peter Pumpkin Head

Why is the church so opposed to atheism? This question is rarely asked, if at all. There are, perhaps, several reasons. The most obvious one is that we are told the lie, repeated so often that it is unquestioned, that society's morality is on the line if we give up faith. This is obvious nonsense. It is evident that religious morality is dubious at best – certainly it is contradictory and muddled. Being willing slaves to a capricious deistic monster is hardly the best way to live but that is exactly how theists who see no harm in mental dictatorship tell us we are supposed to act.

Theists often make the claim that god has given us free will so that we can make our own minds up. Then, of course, they say he will punish us if we don't believe in him. They say their god has given us the ability to think for ourselves but that he punishes us for free thought. Numerous theologians – cheery Martin Luther among them – have stated that believers must crush all reason so that they may know god. *'Give up thinking'*, in other words. This makes a mockery of the idea that god has given us free will. *'Stop thinking and you can believe anything we tell you.'* This is immoral, to say the least.

Is it more likely that those who preach from the pulpit are the ones living in fear? That in their hearts they know it for what it really is? Surely, theologians who take empty degrees in theism must read about the biblical forgeries, the arguments that it's all myth, that most of the characters in the bible didn't exist and have no basis in archaeology or are at best, like Herod who has been re-imagined as a kind of Hollywood villain, gross misrepresentations.

Do theologians fear the dark? (Yes.) Do they fear that the

universe is an amoral place? (It is.) Do they fear that, if humanity was wiped out by natural disaster (or fundamentalist religion), everything would carry on regardless? (It would – without so much as batting the proverbial eyelid.) That we are insignificant on the cosmological scale? (We are.)

The most treasured elements of society are its freedoms and its power of democracy – religion offers neither. Religion is seen as part of the democratic process when it is nothing of the sort. Democracy is not something religious people, particularly at the fundamentalist end of the spectrum, genuinely like. In democracy, we are free to pick and choose but religion, because of the constricting system under which it operates, will not tolerate such freedoms. Theists of all faiths fear the loss of power.

At heart maybe those who shout the most about atheism, science and evolution are the ones who fear that something they believe in may very well turn out to be utter twaddle. (They are right to fear. It is.) Darwinian evolution, which necessarily goes hand in hand with atheism, is one big spotlight to illuminate the dark. That darkness, in the hands of theists, is a powerful tool for compliance.

As Steven Pinker writes in *The Blank Slate*:

> *The religious opposition to evolution is fuelled by*
> *several moral fears. Most obviously, the fact that*
> *evolution challenges the literal truth of the creation*
> *story in the bible and thus the authority religion*
> *draws from it. As one creationist minister put it,*
> *'If the bible gets it wrong in biology, then why*
> *should I trust the bible when it talks about morality*
> *and salvation'…*

The minister shouldn't, of course. The bible is full of immorality, contradiction and savagery. In fact, to draw inspiration for morality from such a flawed work is a dubious practice at best. Any serious theologian, worth their pillar of salt, knows this. To deny this fact is to deny the very substance of a book that defies reason.

As Thomas Paine declared:

> Whenever we read the obscene stories, the voluptuous debaucheries, the cruel and torturous executions, the unrelenting vindictiveness, with which more than half the Bible is filled, it would be more consistent that we called it the word of a demon, than the word of God. It is a history of wickedness, that has served to corrupt and brutalise mankind; and, for my part, I sincerely detest it, as I detest everything that is cruel.

Is it not likely, though, that men in positions of power simply do not want to lose their exulted pontifical posts? Would the Pope or the Archbishop of Canterbury give up their power and wealth and live in caves? Of course not. Why doesn't the Vatican and the Church of England lead by example and sell its stocks, shares and assets and actually make a genuine difference in the world by sharing it with the poor. Surely that is the height of Christian benevolence, the highest moral good.

Theists attempt to fill our minds with strident lies, among them the idea that non-believers perform great evils. Greater evil has been perpetrated by theists (often in collaboration with those they claim to despise) in the name of their myths. They revel in their ability to scare us – they demand conformity through fear. Isn't there something psychologically perverse about that?

Recently, Pope Benedict XVI has been condemning the creeping rejection of Catholicism in South America by using scare tactics about Marxist ideology, which appears to be on the rise as a bulwark against interfering American foreign policy and Papal domination. Being a conservative, the Pope is keen to reassert theistic domination, which he thinks is better for the people. (He has stated that Catholicism is the 'one true way', how so?) As well as claiming, erroneously, that the people were 'silently crying out' for Christianity (such startling hubris and arrogance!), he's resorting to tinkering with history (not the first or last time) and spouting the old and hideously false maxim, *Ecclesia non novit sanguinem* ('the Church is untainted by blood') in an effort to play down the role of the Catholic Church in supporting Conquistadors such as Hernan Cortes, Francisco Pizarro and Diego de Almagro who ravaged the continent and put to death great numbers of the indigenous peoples in the name of Christianity in the sixteenth century. Or the destructive extremism of the fanatical Spanish monk, Diego de Landa, who, after burning many of the priceless books of the Maya, compounded his assault on their culture by becoming interested in their system of writing but in the process making a real and insulting hash of it. The Catholic Church's power base in the continent is under threat and powerful organisations resent rejection. Power and control are at stake.

It may very well be that in this case, as in others in the past, a mixture of theism and politics, god and mammon, has come together in a neo-con, anti-Marxist political manoeuvre to keep an influence over (oil) resources – especially those of Venezuela. Whatever one thinks of Chavez, he is keen to keep foreign interference out of his country. Wouldn't any country want that?

Simply put, many theologians have an all-too-human love of their exalted positions. There is nothing more potent than the combination of god, money and power. Atheism threatens to take that away. There are many theists out there who really do think we have souls and that they are under threat if we disbelieve in the 'sky fairy'. But they are surrendering themselves to archaic fears. We must always ask, what have theists got to lose?

Conclusion

Atheist awakening rouses people all over the world into the feeling of master-ship over their institutions and systems of life. The spread of the atheist outlook is hope of humanity to turn from war to peace, from slavery to freedom, from superstition to a sense of reality, from conflict to cooperation.
Gora, *We Become Atheists*

What has religion ever given us? Some cracking buildings (at what cost?), wonderful art and excellent music and that's about it… oh, and, of course, the slaughter of millions, war and misery…

It has taught us absolutely nothing about the real world or the wider universe. It has brought us nothing that can compare with Darwinian evolution (a universal acid that eats away at bogus concepts), quantum physics, chemistry, archaeology, anthropology, geology and every scientific method that exists. Evolution is not a belief system. It is fact – an observable and testable process subject to intense scrutiny, which, time and time again, resists all attempts to demolish it. We can no more deny evolution than we can stop the Earth from turning. If we accept evolution, as we must, then the idea of divine creation slips further away into the category of wishful thinking where it belongs.

All theists have for evidence to prop up their beliefs are their respective holy books. In reality, this means they have nothing at all. Despite decrying it, theists long for a scientific method to back them up. They yearn for hard proof but they will never have it. Creationists particularly, even though they loathe science, still look forward to the day when it will work for them but it never will. Religion is jealous of science. Science finds answers to the questions it raises. If it doesn't, it keeps going – it does not tarry on its journey. If it's wrong, it either owns up to the mistake or is forced to do so and submits.

Theists labour the point about 'faith' but faith is an empty promise and an insulting concept for humanity. Yet, at the end of the day, although ephemeral and essentially useless, it is all religion has. Faith is nothing more than a theistic admission that evidence for a deity is nowhere to be found. Religion is, by its nature, stagnant, offering nothing to humanity. Religion ties itself into ever-tightening Gordian knots. Atheism is the willing Alexander. Religion is a conceptual dead end, a cul-de-sac for thought. It revels in so-called mysteries where there are none. The splendidly bearded Christopher Howse even has a column in the Daily Telegraph entitled *Sacred Mysteries* but does he really believe there are any? Does he really prefer a world made up of silly empty nonsense? What exactly is a 'sacred mystery' anyway? Atheism sweeps away false hope, delusion and the reliance on the non-existent. It attempts to solve mysteries not revel in them.

> One would think that a system loaded with such gross and vulgar absurdities as scripture religion is, could never have obtained credit; yet we have seen what priestcraft and fanaticism could do, and credulity believe.
>
> Thomas Paine, *The Age of Reason*

Religion bitterly resists rational explanation for, just as in stage magic, once its tricks are explained, it loses its appeal. The audience walk away, knowing they have been duped. Believing in the supernatural does not make us better people and, more importantly, it does not make society better. In fact, it can be the root cause of great injustices and act as an excuse for social ills. The likes of Opus Dei and certain factions of the Catholic Church have themselves backed various dictators around the world, such as Pinochet, yet they decry atheism as the strong-hold of dictators and immorality. Theists should put their own house in order before seeking to lay the blame on others.

It is clear that, in the final analysis, faith is all theists have. To atheists it is a dead loss but to theists it is their last best hope. Debates about angels on the head of a pin or who said what to whom and what it 'really' all means, are bogus. All the dogmatic writings, pontificating, papal bulls, re-reading and re-interpreta-tion of religious books, apocryphal gospels, theological treatises, and messiahs – the whole shoddy edifice is meaningless. Debates on religious mysteries are discussions about nothing. It is all like a theology degree – pointless and, in the end, worthless. Religion may offer comfort in times of stress or personal loss but this is surely nothing more than an escape from reality by immersion in a false narcotic. Why not simply face reality? Theistic apologists assume the best way to defend the untenable is by means of a feeble offensive, using centuries-old and misfiring linguistic weapons. They play the blame game. But where is their god?

> ...The utter and total failure of all religionists in all countries to produce one particle of evidence showing the existence of any supernatural power whatever, and the further fact that the people are not satisfied with their religion. They are continually asking for evidence. They are asking it in every imaginable way. The sects are continually dividing. There is no real religious serenity in the world. All religions are opponents of intellectual liberty, I believe in absolute mental freedom. Real religion with me is a thing not of the head, but of the heart; not a theory, not a creed, but a life.
>
> Robert Ingersoll, from an interview.

Atheism is the proper default state for the mind and it should be backed up with healthy scepticism about the world. It rids the mind of infantile wishes. In engaging with theists what atheism does is come up against fantasy. Atheism may as well enter into a debate with the world of *Star Trek* or *Lord of the Rings*. Rational minds are tackling irrational minds. To engage with theists has no more relevance than dealing with trekkies but at least the latter are more tolerant than rabid theists.

From Lucretius and the Materialists to the Renaissance and then the Enlightenment there have been escalating attempts by humanity to rid itself of the millennia-old shackles of theism, which have often expressed themselves in convulsions of rebellion. Each time there has been a surge of free thought and the chains have been loosened a little more. Since Darwin, humanity has once more felt the liberating ideas of disbelief ripple through it. Darwinian evolution created the long-sought revolution in thought that allowed the atheistic mind to truly flourish. There was a genuine alternative to theistic despotism.

Perhaps now we are at last on the road, complete with Darwinian signposts, to our true potential as a rational species and we are ready to rid ourselves of childish and selfish thoughts so that we can grow up into a universe we can investigate with open minds. We can move beyond the cheap tinsel of beliefs in which we are made slaves to ghosts. We can reach a time when intellectual efforts can concentrate on dealing with the genuine search for truth and need not waste precious time clearing the fog of faith.

> While the (often demented) ideologue will construct a giant, many-mansioned edifice on the shakiest of foundations, the intellectual has the unenviable task of showing up the next day, chisel in hand, in order to chip away – bit by bit – at the house of lies.
>
> Rayyan Al-Shawaf, *eSkeptic*, 9 May 2007

Surely the best way to truth is through honest discovery. Anything else is pure dishonesty and that includes religion with its indulgence in fantasy. Atheism is the way ahead. Religion is born of arrogance, atheism of humility. Nature isn't set up for man's benefit. Atheism demands that we deal with issues in the real world and removes any appeal to some mysterious unseen non-existent entity. It is not our natural state now but, one day, it may become the bedrock of humanity and we will all be the better for it. With the resurgence of tyrannical theism we need desperately to solidify atheism's position as a bulwark against irrationality. Our future may depend on it. The notion of a deity is an insult to humanity and the sooner we realise this the better. We can still be decent moral human beings without resorting to fairy tales. Somehow society looks down on those who refuse to buy into wishful thinking, myths and legends; that the mark of a good citizen is to believe in nonsense. Atheism challenges and destroys that bigotry. Science is always portrayed in terms of Promethean arrogance when it's religion that suffers from inter-minable superiority. There is nothing more arrogant than the idea of a god making man in his image and a universe constructed only for our benefit. Nothing more idiotic than the oafish sentiment of human divinity as if somehow we are the most important beings in the cosmos. Why does a god create an expanding universe so big, that we as a species can never hope to explore in its entirety? Why create the laws of physics then spend time breaking them? Why create the laws of evolution then create humanity at the click of a finger or then insist people believe in a six–day creation? Frankly, it doesn't get any more arrogant than that.

So are five billion or more people wrong about religion? What if five billion people believed the Earth was flat – not only flat but flat in different ways? Should they be respected in their views? And would a minority be wrong to criticise that position? Certainly not.

We need to emasculate the monolithic edifices of religion

that serve only to repress free thought and human potential. Religion grows ever more perverse and destructive as time passes, especially in its connections and influence over international politics, where it reveals its true face. The perverse evidence for god's non-existence is blatantly exposed in the actions of evangelical and fundamentalist lunatics who unleash their bigotry and arrogance through bomb and bullet. Any right thinking individual would move mountains to stop death and destruction in their name – so why doesn't god? Why the howling silence from above when thousands die in his name? Whatever criticisms are made of atheism, we must hold on to the one overriding, obvious and inescapable fact that god is conspicuous by his absence from the universe. We have only to open our eyes to see this.

> *Our civilisation has not yet fully recovered from the shock of its birth – the transition from the tribal, or 'closed society', with its submission to magical forces, to the 'open society', which sets free the critical powers of man.*
> Sir Karl Popper. *The Open Society and its Enemies.*

What do the following people have in common?

Pliny, Lucretius, Bertrand Russell, Isaac Asimov, Fred Hoyle, Ursula K LeGuin, Harlan Ellison, Piers Anthony, Arthur C. Clarke, Marlon Brando, Sir John Gielgud, Peter Ustinov, Penn and Teller, Randy Newman, Noam Chomsky, Gore Vidal, David Hume, Derren Brown, Roger Penrose, Richard Dawkins, Albert Einstein, Nikolai Rimsky-Korsakov, Margaret Sanger, Daniel Dennett, Sam Harris, Francois Mitterand, John Cage, EE Cummings, Allen Ginsberg, James Randi, William Carlos Williams, Ibn Warraq, Karl Marx, John Lennon, Jonathan Miller, Stanley Kubrick…The list goes on and on…

Yes, they all are, or were, non-believers! Not exactly a talent-less group of people – all of them have contributed, as have

countless other atheists, an enormous amount to human understanding and knowledge of the world.

Have a look at Warren Allen Smith's *Who's Who In Hell,* for a
comprehensive list of famous folk who are (or were) freethinkers, secularists, atheists and humanists.

A Few Famous Atheists

David Hume (1711–1776)

David Hume was born in Edinburgh where he would later study law at the university. Failing to graduate and suffering from depression, he worked for a time in Bristol as a counting house clerk. In 1734, he moved to Anjou and wrote *A Treatise of Human Nature,* which he published anonymously in London. It was an extension of the works of John Locke (1632–1704) and George Berkeley (1685–1753). The book failed to make an impact so he followed it with *Essays Moral and Political.* The political economist Adam Smith became an advocate of Hume's work. Hume's atheism meant he was turned down for professorships at Edinburgh and Glasgow Universities. After being a tutor to the almost insane Marquis of Annandale and secretary to General St Clair during various covert missions abroad, he edited the *Treatise of Human Nature* into the more concise book, *An Inquiry Concerning Human Understanding*, which was severely critical of Kant's philosophy.

One of his most famous quotes, and something of a mantra for sceptics and freethinkers, comes from *An Inquiry Concerning Human Understanding*: 'No testimony is sufficient to establish a miracle unless the testimony be of such kind that its falsehood would be more miraculous than the fact which it endeavours to establish.'

Thomas Paine (1737–1809)

Born in Thetford, Paine was the son of a Quaker corset maker. After leaving the family profession, he was a schoolmaster, a sailor and an exciseman but was dismissed from the latter job for demanding better pay. In London, he met Benjamin Franklin who persuaded him to move to America in 1774. In Philadelphia, he became a radical journalist. As the Revolution broke out, he published a pamphlet entitled *Common Sense* (1776), which demanded immediate independence. In 1787, he moved back to England and published *The Rights of Man*. He was accused of treason for his anti-monarchist tracts and for his later role in the French Revolution. In France he supported the moderate Girondins and angered Robespierre by arguing against the execution of the king. In 1794, he published his greatest work *The Age of Reason*, a powerful attack on religion. He was ostracised for his deism or near-atheism and died penniless on his farm at New Rochelle in New York State.

Karl Marx (1818 – 83)

Marx was born in Trier to a Jewish family who converted to Protestantism to avoid anti-Semitism. He studied in the universities of Bonn (1835–1836) and Berlin (1836–1841) where he met up with those influenced by the philosopher Hegel who were critical of religion. After working for a liberal paper, the *Rheinische Zeitung*, which was shut down by a repressive government, he moved to Paris where he wrote his first book *Economic and Philosophical Manuscripts of 1844*. He moved to Brussels and, in collaboration with Friedrich Engels, wrote the *Communist Manifesto* in 1848. After a brief return to Germany, he moved to London where he lived for the rest of his life. There, in the British Library, he wrote his most famous work, *Das Kapital*.

Robert Green Ingersoll (1833–1899)

Robert Ingersoll was born in Dresden, New York State. He became a colonel in the Civil War and then State Attorney-General for Illinois. He was a republican orator who lectured to large crowds about the idiocy of Christian belief and became one of the most important freethinkers and advocates of rationality and reason of his day. He published a number of books on free thought, including *The Gods, and Other Lectures* (1876) and *Why I Am An Agnostic* (1896).

Charles Bradlaugh (1833–1891)

The English social reformer Charles Bradlaugh was born in London and was variously employed as an errand boy, a coal merchant and a soldier. He became a lecturer in secularism in 1853 and wrote pamphlets under the pseudonym 'Iconoclast'. He moved from editor to proprietor of the *National Reformer* in 1862. Being an atheist he was unable to swear the oath of allegiance when he was elected to parliament in 1880 and was expelled repeatedly until 1886 when he reluctantly agreed to take the oath. A decade earlier he had been prosecuted in a notorious trial, together with Annie Besant, for promoting birth control in a leaflet entitled *The Fruits of Philosophy*. In 1876 he took part in a six-day series of debates in the Temperance Hall, Birmingham under the overall title 'Is the Bible Divine?' He wrote numerous atheistic tracts including *A Plea For Atheism* and *What Did Jesus Teach?*

Friedrich Nietzsche (1844–1900)

German philosopher who rejected the slave mentality of Christianity and the idea that there were absolute moral values. He was born in Rocken in Saxony and attended Bonn and Leipzig Universities. He was later professor of Greek at Basel. He rejected theology to study philology. He is famous, among other things, for the statement, 'god is dead' and his books included *Also Sprach Zarathustra* (Thus Spake Zarathustra), *Ecce Homo* (Behold the Man) and *Jenseits von Gutt and Bose* (Beyond Good and Evil). It is claimed that his writings were the precursor to Nazism but, in reality, they are at odds with the ideology of totalitarian regimes. He coined the word and the concept of '*ubermensch*' – '*superman*'.

Sigmund Freud (1856–1939)

Influential Austrian psychoanalyst who pioneered the exploration of the unconscious mind through free association of ideas and dream analysis and changed the way mental illness was treated. Much of his earlier work was focused on repressed sexuality as a basis for neurosis but, latterly, he moved into the study of self-gratification and self-preservation. As an atheist, he thought that religion was an illusion born from neurosis. Like the more mystical Jung, he was one of the most influential names in twentieth century neuropsychology. He wrote *The Interpretation of Dreams* (1900) and *The Ego and Id* (1923).

Joseph McCabe (1867–1955)

Joseph McCabe was a catholic priest who converted to atheism and went on to write more atheistic books than anyone else. He demolished the Catholic Church in such books as *Is the Position of Atheism Growing Stronger? The Forgery of the Old Testament*, *Religious Lies*, *Did Jesus Ever Live?*, *Do We Need Religion?* and *The Value of Scepticism*.

As an example of his writing, we can quote the following:

> The Roman Catholic Church is an anachronism, an imposture, which the world is rapidly finding out... It is poor in scholarship and rich in crime. It hates and fears truth. It still prefers the cloak and dagger, the intrigue and the secret bullying.

Madalyn Murray O'Hair (1919–1995)

Once referred to as the most hated woman in America, Madalyn Murray O'Hair was certainly a controversial figure. She was born Madalyn Mays in Pittsburgh and raised a Presbyterian. She studied law at Ashland College and South Texas College of Law but never took it up as a career. Because of her belligerent attitude she rarely held down a job for long and she often came into conflict with the authorities, especially over her successful legal challenge to public prayer and bible reading in schools. The United States Supreme Court voted in her favour. Shortly after this success, she founded American Atheists to protect the rights of freethinkers and filed many lawsuits to separate church from state. In 1995 she, her son and granddaughter went missing in suspicious circumstances. An apathetic police force hardly stirred itself to solve the mystery. David Waters, a convicted felon, later admitted to murdering them. Critics of O'Hair said she was not exactly the best advert for atheism in America. Theists often showed unseemly delight over her death and they now use her frequently as an example of how corrupt atheism supposedly is.

In a speech entitled '*Atheism*', O'Hair wrote the following:

All conventional religions are based on idealism. Many varieties of idealism exist, but the apologist for idealism and opponents of materialism go under many names; we have, for instance, dualists, objective idealists, subjective idealists, solipsists, positivists, Machians, irrationalists, existentialists, neo-positivists, logical positivists, fideists, revived medieval scholastics, Thomists. And opposed to these stand alone the Atheistic materialists (or perhaps naturalists, Rationalists, freethinkers, etc.) who have no need for intellectual machinations, deceptions, or masquerades.

Bertrand Russell (1872–1970)

Russell was born in Monmouthshire. He studied mathematics and philosophy at Trinity College, Cambridge and wrote the *Principia Mathematica* in which he argued that mathematics could be seen as a branch of logic. He was an outspoken liberal pacifist and was jailed for his beliefs after writing an article for a pacifist publication. He was later fired from an American university because of his liberal morality. After World War Two, he was actively involved in the campaign for nuclear disarmament. He won the Nobel Prize for literature in 1950. His many and varied writings included *Why I am Not a Christian* and *Sceptical Essays*.

Richard Dawkins (1941–)

Born in Nairobi, Richard Dawkins has become one of the most pre-eminent atheists in contemporary thought. He first came to prominence in 1976 with his book *The Selfish Gene*, which became a best seller. Since then he has written several highly influential books including *The Extended Phenotype*, *Climbing Mount Improbable*, *Unweaving the Rainbow* and the ripsnorting *The God Delusion*. He has made several documentaries about Darwinian evolution and the recent, highly recommended *The Root Of All Evil?* He is the Charles Simonyi Professor for the

Public Understanding of Science at Oxford University. See also the Richard Dawkins Foundation for Science and Reason.

Sam Harris (1967–)

Harris is the author of the must-read books *The End of Faith* (2004) and *Letter to a Christian Nation* (2006). He writes extensively about the threat to secular society from tolerance of religious faith. If we are to progress, we must stop being subservient to political correctness when it comes to belief. Society is being damaged by religion and our attitudes to it. In other words, we are being too tolerant of idiotic ideas. Secular moderation is the root cause of religious extremism – with many feeling too fearful to speak out in critical terms about any religion, particularly, in the present climate, Islam. Harris, like all freethinkers, knows that religion, as a source of morality, is a bogus concept.

Glossary

Agnosticism

The belief that the existence or non-existence of god or gods cannot be proved either way. It cannot be confirmed or denied. Agnostics are fence sitters. The term was invented by TH Huxley. Agnostics can be either atheistic-agnostic or theistic-agnostic. There are two kinds of agnosticism: TAP – Temporary Agnosticism in Practice and PAP – Permanent Agnosticism in Principle. See Dawkins, *The God Delusion*.

Anthropic Principle

The arrogant pseudo-scientific idea that humans are important to the existence and the observation of the universe. It is split into the Weak Anthropic Principle – that for the universe to be observed it must be structured in such a way as to facilitate this – and the Strong Anthropic Principle – that the universe must have inherent properties, which allow life to develop at some point in its history. There is also the Final Anthropic Principle and the Participatory Principle, which states that life, when created, will change the universe to ensure its immortality. Devised by theists, Barrow and Tipler, it attacks the Copernican Principle that humanity is insignificant and has no role in an amoral universe. It has been roundly demolished. See *Why People Believe Weird Things* by Michael Shermer and *The God Delusion* by Richard Dawkins for critiques.

Atheism

Non-belief or free thought. An atheist denies the existence of a deity or deities and that reality has a supernatural element to it. Atheism is the base line for rational thought. There are five kinds of atheism. Dogmatic atheism – there definitely is no god; sceptical atheism – the mind is not good enough to deduce whether or not there is a god; critical atheism – which says that the evidence for god is inadequate; philosophical atheism – the failure to find any evidence of god; and speculative atheism – impossibility of demonstrating there is a god. Atheism is not a belief but the absence of belief.

Deism

Someone who believes that a divine intelligence, of whatever form, kickstarted the universe and then sat back to play no more part in its running. Deism sometimes refers to a mode of thought prevalent in the seventeenth and eighteenth centuries – a religion of nature. God is the source of natural law but it's up to man to make the most of it.

Humanism

The belief in the potential of humanity if it rejects the supernatural. Humanity has the ability to improve itself through its own efforts and secular morality.

Monotheism

The belief in one god only. The Abrahamic religions of Christianity, Islam and Judaism are all monotheistic.

NOMA (Non Overlapping Magisteria)

Ridiculous term coined by the otherwise eminent American biologist Stephen J. Gould which states that the realms of science and religion are necessarily to be kept apart. Science deals with the material world while religion has sole dominion over ethics, morality and the meaning of life. NOMA is a sop to religion. No realm is beyond science.

Pantheism

From the Greek words *pan* ('all') and *theos* ('god'). Pantheism is the idea that all of reality is divine and that god is present in all of nature. The major religions can be interpreted as being pantheistic as well as those of ancient Egypt, Brahmanism, stoicism and Neoplatonism.

Polytheism

Is the belief in more than one god. The most famous examples of polytheistic societies are the Egyptians, Romans, and the Greeks, although nearly all cultures have been at one time or another polytheistic. It predates monotheism.

Secularism

Term coined by George Jacob Holyoake. Secularists are

concerned with the activities of the real world and do not accept any notion of the supernatural or religious. Secularisation is the giving up of religious practices as industrialisation, science and knowledge about the real world develop in a society.

Theism

Someone who believes that a deity, or deities, takes an active part in the day-to-day running of the universe and that through special appeals can be asked to intervene in a situation. Theism boils down to nothing more than the ephemeral term 'faith' – in effect, an admission that there is no evidence.

Utilitarianism

System of ethics outlined by Jeremy Bentham (1748–1836), James Mill (1773–1836) and John Stuart Mill (1806–73) which states that if an action is morally right it leads to happiness, if wrong unhappiness. Society should therefore strive for the greatest happiness of the greatest number. It is a variation of *consequentialism* – the belief that the morality of the action is judged by its consequences. This is in sharp contrast to the beliefs of moral absolutists who think that there are absolutes of right and wrong.

Bibliography
(MUST HAVE BOOKS IN THE ATHEIST'S LIBRARY)

Baggini, Julian, *Atheism: A Very Short Introduction*, Oxford: Oxford University Press, 2003

Barker, Dan, *Losing Faith in Faith: From Preacher to Atheist*, Madison, WI: Freedom from Religion Foundation, 1992

Dawkins, Richard, *The God Delusion*, London: Transworld, 2006

Drange, Theodore M, *Nonbelief and Evil: Two Arguments for the Nonexistence of God*, New York: Prometheus, 1998

Gould, Stephen J., *The Mismeasure of Man*, New York: WW Norton, 1981

Grayling, AC, *What Is Good?: The Search for the Best Way to Live*, London: Weidenfeld & Nicolson, 2003

Harbour, Daniel, *An Intelligent Person's Guide to Atheism*, London: Duckworth, 2001

Harris, Sam, *The End of Faith*, London: Simon & Schuster, 2006

Harris, Sam, *Letter to a Christian Nation*, London: Bantam Press, 2007

Hitchens, Christopher, *God is Not Great: How Religion Poisons Everything*, London: Atlantic Books, 2007

Krueger, Douglas E., *What is Atheism?: A Short Introduction*, New York: Prometheus, 1998

Le Poidevin, Robin, *Arguing for Atheism: An Introduction to the Philosophy of Religion*, London: Routledge, 1996

Paine, Thomas, *The Age of Reason*, New York: Dover Publications, 2004

Russell, Bertrand, *Why I Am Not a Christian*, London: Routledge, 2004

Sagan, Carl, *The Demon-Haunted World: Science as a Candle in the Dark*, New York: Random House, 1995

Shelley, Percy Bysshe, *The Necessity of Atheism*, New York: Prometheus, 1993

Shermer, Michael, *How We Believe: The Search for God in an Age of Science*, New York: WH Freeman, 1999

Smith, George E., *Atheism: The Case Against God*, New York: Prometheus, 1979

Stein, Dr. Gordon, *The Encyclopedia of Unbelief*, New York: Prometheus, 1985

Stenger, Victor, *God: The Failed Hypothesis*, New York: Prometheus, 2007

Wheen, Francis, *How Mumbo Jumbo Conquered the World*, London: Fourth Estate, 2004

Prometheus Books, set up by Paul Kurtz in New York in 1970, several of whose titles feature in the above list, are well worth investigating. They are publishers of numerous critically acclaimed books on freethought, scepticism and disbelief.

Some Websites of Interest

American Atheists:
www.atheists.org

Atheist Alliance International:
www.atheistalliance.org

The Brights:
www.the-brights.net

British Humanist Association:
www.humanism.org.uk

Darwin On Line:
www.darwin-online.org.

International Humanist and Ethical Union – UK:
www.iheu.org/

James Randi Educational Foundation:
www.randi.org

National Secular Society:
www.secularism.org.uk/

Rationalist Press Association:
www.rationalist.org.uk/

Richard Dawkins Foundation for Science and Reason:
www.richarddawkins.net

The Skeptics Society:
www.skeptic.com

Index